Chiricahua Apache Women and Children

NUMBER TWENTY-ONE
Elma Dill Russell Spencer
Series in the West and Southwest

Chiricahua Apache Women and Children

Safekeepers of the Heritage

H. HENRIETTA STOCKEL

Texas A&M University Press
College Station

The paper used in this book
meets the minimum requirements
of the American National Standard
for Permanence of Paper for Printed
Library Materials, z39.48-1984.
Binding materials have been
chosen for durability.

Library of Congress Cataloging-in-Publication Data

Stockel, H. Henrietta, 1938–
    Chiricahua Apache women and children :
safekeepers of the heritage / H. Henrietta Stockel.
        p.   cm. — (Elma Dill Russell Spencer series
in the West and Southwest ; no. 21)
    Includes bibliographical references and index.
    ISBN 0-89096-921-3 (cloth)
    1. Chiricahua women—History.   2. Chiricahua
women—Social life and customs.   3. Chiricahua
children—Social conditions. I. Title. II. Series.
E99.C68 S76   2000
305.48'897—dc21   99-047761
                                                  CIP

CONTENTS

ILLUSTRATIONS

PREFACE

This is a time in my career when I have acquired enough information about Chiricahua Apache culture and history, particularly as it concerns the women, to be asked to speak on the topic to history, civic, academic, library, and women's groups, students, Elderhostels, and many others. I welcome these opportunities for I have set a course for myself that is based in telling the truth about the Chiricahuas to as many people as possible. Because these speaking engagements are becoming more and more frequent, my goal is gradually being reached, and that is most satisfying. Of course, I will never reach everyone, and that is fine, as long as the interested people who attend my lectures have a fuller appreciation of the Apaches and are truthfully informed. Eve Ball (*Indeh: An Apache Odyssey* and *In the Days of Victorio,* among others) and Dan Thrapp (*The Conquest of Apacheria* and *Victorio and the Mimbres Apaches,* among others) were my mentors and just as they told the truth about Geronimo's people in their books and their discussions, so will I.

When I address groups and am inevitably asked if I am a Chiricahua Apache, my truthful answer is "No." I was born into an Austrian-Danish family in New Jersey, received an education in the public schools and went on, after a delay, to enroll in Columbia University. When both parents were dead and I was in my mid-thirties, I left the East and landed in Santa Fe, New Mexico, with two cats, one suitcase, no job, and no friends to await my presence in the great American Southwest. Left behind deliberately because of the irresistible lure of Apache-dom were my friends, family, and the myriad of professional opportunities that could have come with advanced academic degrees. Some may call it a midlife crisis. I called it fulfilling a dream.

I had been intrigued, nay, obsessed, by Geronimo's people since I was a girl of about ten and saw a John Wayne movie. In the film, the name of which I have forgotten, he was a cavalry officer sitting atop a horse spying on a band of Indians riding in a dust cloud along the valley far below the mesa. Thanks to camera techniques, we kids in the theater audience that Saturday afternoon saw exactly what he saw through his telescope: an actor impersonating Geronimo, wearing a full Sioux feathered headdress, leading a pack of the worst-looking actors playing Apache warriors that the casting company could find. Nonetheless, I was a goner when Wayne turned to his cavalry men with a look of fear on his face and muttered, "Geronimo!" From that moment on, the Chiricahua Apaches were part of my life, so much so that my mother nicknamed me her "Indian child."

Eve Ball understood and shared her extensive information with me when I contacted her in Ruidoso several months after arriving in New Mexico. Off and on we sat for a number of years in the same room in which, decades previously, the Chiricahua leaders Asa Daklugie, Eugene Chihuahua, James Kaywaykla, and others sat with her and told her about their heritage. I felt privileged to rest on the same chair Daklugie did and to be able to ask Eve what I thought were intelligent questions. She always answered as if I were her peer, which God knows I was not and still am not, but she never patronized, never mocked, and never downplayed the seriousness of my interest. Neither did Dan Thrapp when I visited him after Eve had passed on, and I had begun to write and publish on my own. Dan once showed me some bullet casings he had found at Tres Castillos, the site of Victorio's death. He had them mounted, and as he took the frame off the wall of his study to give me a closer look, I saw tears in his eyes. We wept together at the tragedy. Dan always expressed great interest in my stated wish to some day write about the impact of Christianity on the Chiricahua Apaches, a project now at long last underway. I am sad that neither he nor Eve will see the fruits of that long, long labor of my love. I am, nonetheless, continually inspired by them and am convinced that both of them somewhere and somehow know what I am currently writing.

My own adventures among the Chiricahua Apaches started when I telephoned the minister at the Dutch Reformed Church on the reservation for an appointment and he agreed. I drove the two hundred miles in what seemed to be a speed akin to slow motion. After chatting pleasantly for a while about the pastor's successes in creating and sustaining a youth group, he pointed out the Cultural Center and directed me to the curator, Elbys Hugar. Of course I knew the name. She was the great-granddaughter of Cochise. I met her that day and returned to the reservation for many subsequent sessions in which she spoke candidly about her heritage and her life. Just like that. She invited me to attend a ceremony in Anadarko, Oklahoma, at the National Hall of Fame for Famous American Indians in which a sculptured bronze bust of Cochise was to be entered. I made the trip during an August week when the temperature was over one hundred degrees and the humidity not far behind. In Anadarko I first met the woman who would become my "Chiricahua Apache mother," Mildred Cleghorn, a well-regarded national Indian leader who had been named American Indian of the Year.

Mildred Cleghorn was then the chairperson of the Fort Sill Chiricahua/Warm Springs Apache Tribe, headquartered in Apache, Oklahoma. I knew about her too from Eve Ball but was so impressed at seeing her in the flesh that I could not walk up and introduce myself. That was left to my companion, Louise Fairchild, to do. Said Louise, "She and I both have gray hair, so she'll understand when I tap her on the shoulder and say 'hello.'" It worked, and, at Mildred's immediate invitation, we checked out of our motel and checked into her home, where for the next ten years or so we stayed every time we went to Oklahoma. Just like that.

Mildred's cousin, Kathleen Kanseah, who lived on the reservation at Mescalero, was also in Anadarko for Cochise's induction, and we met her at the same time. As Louise and I stood talking near the spot under a tree where Kathleen had perched on an aluminum chair, she reached out her hand. I took it, and she said, "I'm Kathleen. Pull up a chair." Just like that.

Ruey Darrow is another cousin whom we met in Anadarko that year and who now has become the chairperson of the Oklahoma Chiricahuas. She too offered her friendship instantly, and it remains strong and secure despite the miles between Oklahoma and Arizona and only annual get-togethers.

At my talks I tell my audiences all this because most people are curious as to how I have acquired my information that so often seems to combine personal observation and academic study. I continue to research and read and nearly memorize every morsel of credible material I can find about the Chiricahua Apaches and attend all of the tribe's gatherings that I reasonably can. When I lived in New Mexico it was somewhat easier to cover the distances between Santa Fe/Albuquerque and the reservation, or drive the five hundred miles to Apache, Oklahoma. Now that I live in southeastern Arizona—right in sight of Cochise's Stronghold in Apacheria—travel takes a bit longer and has to be planned in advance. Nonetheless, wild horses could not keep me away.

I have been called an "authority" on the Chiricahua Apaches and maybe I am by now, having written several books about various aspects of my favorite subject, but no one born outside the culture can truly claim to know all there is to know. These days I am particularly interested in the period that pre-dates the Chiricahuas' first contact with Anglo Americans. Back in the late 1500s and early 1600s the newcomer Spaniards first tried to impose their way of life on these Apaches and failed. The Mexicans, after independence, also tried and did somewhat better than the Europeans, probably because the Apaches had already tasted the liquor available on the frontier. I am intensely curious about the identities of these early Chiricahuas who so ably and strongly resisted the efforts made to "civilize" them. As we all have learned, however, it was up to the Anglos to subdue this mighty people. Although the history books infer this was accomplished with Geronimo's final surrender in 1886, I disagree. In my opinion, nothing known to humankind has yet been able to conquer the unwavering Chiricahua Apache spirit. Amen.

As for myself and my close companion, Louise Fairchild, if the fates allow, we will continue to nurture the friendships that started so many years ago in New Mexico and Oklahoma and have continued today. Each year brings more friends in our circle and a growing knowledge of the culture and respect for the people. In all my books I have acknowledged Louise's presence in my life and she continues still as my *sine qua non*. And so, for her and for all the Chiricahuas, I offer this book as a small sample of my love and regard. As readers will quickly note, this book is somewhere between a full-blown ethnohistorical monograph and an almost personal memoir. That suits me just fine for most times I feel like I am also in between worlds—the Apache and the Anglo. To tell the truth, I prefer the Chiricahua Apache way. As I have most of my life.

H. Henrietta Stockel
Hereford, Arizona
Apacheria

INTRODUCTION

Strange as it may seem to some, I want to begin this book about Apache women and children by discussing Chiricahua Apache men, and for a good reason: they are better known and thus can serve as the perfect subjects to introduce their women. In American Indian history it has been difficult to surpass the celebrity (or notoriety) of such famous Chiricahua Apaches as Mangas Coloradas, Cochise, Victorio, Nana, Loco, Geronimo, and Chihuahua. The bold strokes of these leaders should be familiar, having been documented, sensationalized, glamorized, embellished, and often, not quite accurately, depicted in films. Contributing to the lore are hundreds of photos, newspaper accounts, and handwritten reports that date back hundreds of years, and writings by many contemporary authors. Nearly all of this material was recorded by non-Indians who provided little or no information about the Chiricahua side of raiding, warfare, and all the other behaviors—militant and peaceful alike—at which the Apache men and women excelled. Eve Ball was among the first of a very few authors to document the Chiricahua perspective. At the time James Kaywaykla, Asa Daklugie, and Eugene Chihuahua[1] talked with her, two of the men were the adult sons of chiefs[2] and the other was the son of a woman warrior. How Mrs. Ball, a diminutive, frail, old-fashioned Southern lady with a thick accent, convinced these three Chiricahuas and others to talk with her for years and years about themselves and their tribe's experiences remains one of the coups in literature about the peoples of the historical American West.

Throughout Eve's book the nearly thirty years of imprisonment of the Chiricahua Apaches by the United States government are mentioned frequently. From September, 1886, with the surrender of Geronimo and his followers, until some time in 1914, the people were incarcerated in Florida, Alabama, and Oklahoma. They lost many of their sacred ceremonies and traditional customs because the authorities prohibited their practice. Their health suffered terribly. Of the 535 men, women, and children initially incarcerated, almost 350 Apaches died, mainly from tuberculosis. With a high death rate and low birth rate, the population of the group was just more than 200 at the time of release from confinement in 1913–14. Almost equally as deplorable, the impact that the imprisonment had upon subsequent generations of Chiricahuas has been devastating; some Chiricahuas will tell you that the tribe as a whole has not recovered yet. Others will not discuss it all. Although many books and films concentrate on the Apache wars, the imprisonment period of Chiricahua history is seldom addressed. Consequently, many people know that Geronimo surrendered, but fewer are aware of what happened next. Fewer still know the consequences of that black period.[3]

Also overlooked by most writers have been the duties and experiences of the historical Chiricahua Apache women and the significant influences they exerted within the family. After all, at the end of the day the mighty warriors and hunters had to come home to their women and children. What were they like? Who were they? The women's roles in relation to their husbands and children, to their relatives, extended families, and to the band or tribe at large were prescribed by inviolable traditions and deserve to be preserved in writing. I hope this book will clearly describe some of those functions. I will devote one chapter to four women warriors whose lifestyle differed substantially from the traditional women's ways. And then Mildred Cleghorn will enter and conclude the book. Some readers will be familiar with her name—or even with her—for she was the chairperson of the Fort Sill Chiricahua/ Warm Springs Apache Tribe in Oklahoma for nearly twenty years and a nationally known dollmaker. More, she was my close friend and my "Apache mother." Born a prisoner of war in 1910, Mrs. Cleghorn lived a long life and died in a tragic 1997 automobile accident.

Although modern Apache women's lifestyles have been influenced by their tribe's history, and thus substantially modified through time, one may yet glimpse, in some of these women, visions of the long ago. For example, tradition states that the bear is considered to be an evil animal and any contact at all with one must be neutralized or a serious disease or broken bones will occur. Several years ago I went to a hunting lodge high in the mountains with Apache friends. As we waited for a table in the dining room I saw a stuffed bear standing upright in a corner of the room. I walked over to it to get a closer look and suddenly felt a hand on my arm, pulling me away. "You know better than that," said Kathleen Kanseah, a modern, educated, and well-respected Chiricahua woman leader on the reservation.

For the last decade or so I have had the good fortune to be included in a few Chiricahua women's friendship circles, to participate with them in sacred ceremonies, and to be accepted as a family member without too many restrictions. This privilege humbles me time and time again, particularly as I dance among Apache women around the bonfire at ancient puberty ceremonies. I can remember years ago when I was awkward and ill at ease, unable to catch on to the skip-shuffle step, but eager to respect the invitation to participate in that activity. I recall standing in the glow of firelight on the Mescalero Apache Reservation's sacred dance grounds some distance from Mildred Cleghorn. She was then still the long-time chairperson of her tribe and had come to New Mexico, as she did every year, specifically to see the puberty ceremony and visit with her relatives and friends during the four-day ritual. Although advanced in years, she effortlessly led the line of dancing women all wrapped in their shawls—a time-honored tradition among Chiricahua women. At that time I did not own a shawl—never had reason to wear one. The wraps worn by the women I saw that night were of modern fabrics and bright colors with golden fringe. Many looked purposefully designed, lovingly crafted to commemorate an occasion, remember a loved one, or were a gift from a dear friend or family member. I decided then that I would search for a shawl for myself and look at it from time to time at home to remember the beauty of the Apache women circling the fire. Well, I found a good-looking shawl, and over the years it received more exposure than I expected it would. After my first invitation to participate in the dance, extended by Mildred Cleghorn at the Cochise induction celebration, I packed my shawl to take to every appropriate Chiricahua Apache occasion and danced around the bonfire whenever the opportunity came my way. I continue to do that.

In my younger years I was quite athletic, having been raised with a bunch of neighborhood boys. My favorite sport became tennis and on strong, muscular legs for hours I could chase and hit that little fuzzy ball from one side of the court to another without becoming fatigued. However, after dancing two or four times around the sacred fire behind Mildred Cleghorn and other Chiricahua women, I was ready to fall into a chair. Occasionally I still react that way, but now I have a reason.

I was diagnosed with breast cancer in 1995 and received high doses of chemotherapy every three weeks for six months. To help me endure the intravenous infusions, I wore my shawl in the chemotherapy room and, as the yellow liquid full of poison chemicals ran into my vein, recalled the sound of Apache drums, the voices of male singers, blazing bonfires, and Mildred (as she was called by everyone). One of the memories I concentrated on in that hospital room is of a cold day in September, 1989, at the tribal complex in Apache, Oklahoma, when Mildred set her shawl aside and wore a blue Pendleton blanket to dance. It was a beautiful piece of work, with her name sewn in gold just above the hem, and had been presented to her in honor of her many achievements. Later, when I asked her to tell me more about it, and about the honor it commemorated, she demurred. In typical Apache woman fashion, she switched the subject to a discussion about making fringe for shawls.

With Mildred and several other Chiricahua women, I have attended and participated in puberty ceremonies many times as an observer and as an occasional helper on the Mescalero Apache Reservation. Some of the women have allowed me to assist them in their outdoor cooking arbors as they prepare the ceremonial meals that accompany the rituals. Afterward, I have prayed with them in the ancient way, have danced around the bonfire with them wearing my shawl, and have been blessed by more than one medicine man in traditional and moving ceremonies. By giving me their permission to participate in the ceremonies, through the years the women have acknowledged my sincerity in learning about their rich heritage. I am most thankful.

A brief word of clarification before we begin. My use of the generic word "Apache" throughout this book refers only to the Chiricahua Apaches. If other Apache groups are mentioned, I will specifically designate them by their band names, e.g., Western Apaches, San Carlos or White Mountain Apaches, Mescalero Apaches, and so forth. This is an important *caveat,* for members of the various Apache bands may be closely related, and their ceremonies and language may be similar. However, my knowledge and experience are exclusively about and with the Chiricahua Apaches, and that is what I will convey to readers.

Chiricahua Apache Women and Children

CHAPTER I

Beginnings

Creation myths form the center of a system of tenets in most existing societies.[1] These tales make things seem plausible to the people who hear them; they satisfy; they interpret.[2] These stories about beginnings do not have to be logical, and they do not have to be similar, but they all have been handed down from the elders through the generations. In most cultures, time-honored creation myths do not necessarily coincide with any anthropological, geological, archeological, or historical data. On the contrary, these legends do not require evidence as proof; they just live in the hearts and minds of a people through the centuries and are testimony to the enduring power of language to mold and shape belief.

Anna Birgitta Rooth, an anthropologist, excerpted three hundred creation myths from North American Indian literature. Of these, there were eight different types, and, reducing the number even more, one of these—the sky father and earth mother—was found among the tribes living in southern California, Arizona, and New Mexico, and another one—the emergence—was limited to the Southwest. In the former, a goddess of earth gives birth to all things, and in the latter, "Men, animals, and vegetation live in a cave in the earth . . . When the earth is ready they emerge and begin their wanderings to their present sites . . . a hero is sent to lead them out into the sun from the dark narrow cave where they have lived in misery."[3]

Chiricahua Apache creation myths define and explain where the people came from, how they got where they are, and what happened after that. Major figures in these tales such as the cultural heroine known as White Painted Woman and her son Child-of-the-Water do not, under any circumstances, compete with *Ussen,* the Giver of Life, the One acknowledged by the Chiricahuas to be all powerful and the One to whom all honor and reverence as the ultimate deity is given. *Ussen* is thought of as the creator, the maker of world and people, and the source of all supernatural power. Since the creation, however, this Giver of Life has had little direct contact with humankind. Morris Opler, one of the early writers on the Chiricahua Apaches, reports, "One might say that this deity has been invoked to lend conceptual wholeness to the supernatural world of the Apache."[4]

Myths about *Ussen* are much rarer than those about White Painted Woman and Child-of-the-Water. These two icons justify and explain some of the most important Apache beliefs and rituals. In that way legends about them are more serious than stories about Coyote, a trickster whose misadventures amuse everyone, adults and children alike. Coyote is an unscrupulous character whose adventures sometimes dramatically violate Apache morals and as a consequence lead to disasters. On the other hand, sometimes Coyote acts in a responsible way, such as when he steals fire and spreads it across the world for warmth. Children learn from Coyote tales that animals [and people] can be both good and bad, or, more formally, "Ambiguities and contradictions in Coyote's character possibly reflect Apache knowledge that the same ambiguities and contradictions exist in humans . . . parents and other adults use the traditional myths and tales to educate Apache children . . . Stories about Coyote . . . are used to teach children about the consequences of misguided behavior. Thoughtless and immoral behavior is contrasted implicitly (or explicitly in the asides of a skilled narrator) with the correct Apache way."[5] As Opler wrote in another book, "Gluttony, lying, theft, adultery, incest, and all the other faults and foibles were introduced by Coyote and have become inescapable for those who 'follow Coyote's trail.'"[6]

Other stories relate events in Chiricahua pre-history. One tale describes the earliest of times, even before there were good people on the earth. At that time Giver of Life sent a flood to wash away the badness. After that it rained hard for a long while. When the rain stopped, Child-of-the-Water and White Painted Woman made human beings. Another story about a flood tells of only one mountain that was not entirely covered by water. No human beings lived through this disastrous flood, but there was a rooster that floated on the water and landed atop the mountain.[7] How the rooster procreated and how people repopulated the earth after the water receded is not explained in that particular legend, but it might be that human beings were made from mud figures by Child-of-the-Water.[8] Because there is not just one way humans came into being, a listener can choose favorites.

Geronimo, for example, liked a myth that told of a time in the long ago when there was a battle between the birds and the beasts over light and darkness. The birds wanted light; the beasts preferred darkness. The birds won, but only a few human beings remained alive after the battle. One of them was White Painted Woman. Years later she gave birth to a son whom she hid in a cave to protect him from the only beast still alive—a dragon. The boy almost lost his life when he came face to face with the dragon, but he killed the beast with a bow and arrows and was then named Apache.[9] Tradition states that all Chiricahuas come from this boy.

Opler recorded another version of the birds versus beasts battle. According to what he learned, when Coyote opened a bag containing darkness, it slipped out and spread all over the world. All the creatures who prefer the night loved it, but birds and harmless little animals desired daylight. They played a game to restore the light, with the understanding that the victors could dispatch the vanquished. The birds won the contest and light came to the eastern horizon. A few of the losers got away—the snake, the owl, and the bear. These are still considered to be dangerous, and a great deal of mythology swirls around them.[10]

Other authors as well as Opler have documented the many stories that comprise the core of Chiricahua Apache beliefs. Eve Ball, for example, recorded Warm Springs Chiricahua Apache James Kaywakla's recollections of stories about White Painted Woman.

From earliest youth I knew of White Painted Woman and her Son, Child of the Waters. She was a woman of beauty and chastity. All men admired her but she refused to marry. A prolonged drought brought on a famine and many perished of hunger. As long as she had food she shared it. But a time came when without the miracle of rain nobody could survive. There was a legend that the people might be saved by a virgin willing to sacrifice her life to save theirs. White Painted Woman decided to make that sacrifice. She went from her people and lay upon a rock awaiting death. In the night rain fell upon her and a child was conceived. Because He had no earthly father, people called Him Child of the Waters for He was the Son of Ussen . . . All agree that this Child was sacred. White Painted Woman had constantly to protect Him from the attempts . . . that sought His death. She dug a secret place and built a fire over the entrance. When danger threatened she hid the Child in this cave. When it was safe, she let him out to exercise.[11]

Of the many legends Chiricahua Apache children learn about White Painted Woman, one important tale relates how she developed the rules for the girls' puberty ceremony—an ancient ritual at the core of Chiricahua culture. First of all, the story tells, she bore a child through the power of *Ussen* and named him Child-of-the-Water. His uncle, Killer-of-Enemies, was White Painted Woman's brother. *Ussen* told this man to leave his sister and take one grain of corn to plant. He told Child-of-the-Water and White Painted Woman that they and the Chiricahua Apaches must live on yucca fruit, piñon nuts, and all the other wild plants. After the separation, White Painted Woman said, "From here on we will have the girl's puberty rite. When the girls first menstruate you shall have a feast. There shall be songs for these girls. During this feast the *Gahe* [masked dancers] shall dance in front. After that there shall be round dancing and face to face dancing."[12]

From this simple instruction, an elaborate ritual has been developed that has lasted from the beginning of time until today. Each Fourth of July weekend on the Mescalero Apache Reservation in south-central New Mexico several young women mark their rite of passage into womanhood with a public puberty ceremony, attended by hundreds of Indians and non-Indians. Additionally, private puberty ceremonies are also held at various times during the year, but attendance at those is usually restricted. In the last few years, there has been an increase in the number of young women participating in both the public and private ceremonies—a strong sign that traditional Apache values are still being respected.

Although each year brings something unique to the ritual, one constant remains: the initial sight is breathtaking. Rounding a curve on the highway that bisects the Mescalero Apache Reservation one suddenly sees a hill populated by tall tipis with lodgepoles poking at the sky. Nearby are many acres of brush arbors, one after another, most covered by bright blue tarps. To the right a stadium with huge lights juts out of the hillside. Below and to the left of the arena are dozens of RVs, and to the right, across a narrow winding dirt road, horse trailers are parked and horses of every breed, color, and shape are tied to trees, awaiting Indian rodeo competition in the stadium—one of the adjuncts to the ceremony. A traveler unfamiliar with this annual celebration may only wonder what the occasion is, and keep driving. But the Indian community in New Mexico and elsewhere knows what the Fourth of July weekend means on the reservation. It is a time for enjoying traditional foods, attending the annual rodeo and parade, watching the daily Indian dance contests, and renewing old acquaintances. Most of all, however, it is the time of year when the traditional puberty ceremony is held and when the *Gah'e*, nowadays called the Mountain Spirit Dancers, dance for hours and hours at night around a blazing bonfire.[13]

Myth and reality converge on these *Gah'e*, with regard to their powers. One tale tells of two children—one legless and one blind—who tried to follow their people but could not keep up the pace. The Mountain Spirits appeared and took the children to their home in the mountains and held a ceremony for them. The children were cured and returned to their parents as whole beings. A true-to-life attempted healing by the *Gah'e* occurred during the imprisonment at Fort Marion, Florida, in 1886. A child was gravely ill and needed the assistance of the Mountain Spirit Dancers to survive. Fortunately, the dancers had brought their paint with them into incarceration and prepared their bodies with the sacred colors. Each man was painted a basic green-brown, with yellow on each arm and an insignia in yellow on his back and breast. Each held two wands ornamented with representations of blue lightning. The child was inside a tent in the northwestern section of the fort so the dancers performed their age-old steps in that area first. They charged around, stabbed at the air with their wands, and stomped their feet on the bricks, all in an effort to drive the evil spirits away. At the correct time, the mother held her sick baby up toward them. The *Gah'e* swooshed their holy batons around, over, under, and upon the cradleboard that held the baby as the mother turned her child toward the four directions. Each of the dancers in turn took the child in his hands, pressed the baby to his breast, lifted the cradleboard to the sky, lowered it to the earth, and turned to the four directions. The child's mother and her friends simultaneously pierced the night with shrieks, trills, and ululations.[14] There is no record of whether that child recovered, but if not, the best effort had been made, given the fact that no supplemental healing herbs, such as the people knew while in the Southwest, were available in the different environment.

Dancing by the *Gah'e* at the puberty ceremony, however, is not designed to heal. Instead, the dancers "take a break" so to speak from their other duties and dance in honor of the maidens whose ritual it is. They have been hired by the girls' families, sometimes months in advance of the actual ritual.

At least a year before a girl's puberty ceremony, she either expresses her wish to go through the rite or is asked about it by her family [traditionally, when menstruation begins]. Her positive response sets into motion an entire process that returns to White Painted Woman's instructions. Interestingly, in the 1800s, if a girl began to menstruate during the time the people were avoiding their enemies, the flight halted for a brief time in order to hold the ceremony. I was told by a Chiricahua elder that their foes never came near when the people stopped to conduct the ceremony, regardless of how close in the pursuit the armies of both countries—the United States and Mexico—were.[15]

As you can see from only this one illustration, the importance of this ritual cannot be underestimated, and I will address it in detail in a subsequent chapter. But for now I will begin by discussing the duties of Apache women, their social standing, and then the birth of a girl child.

CHAPTER 2

The Way They Were

Along with lessons contained in creation myths and other stories, women's activities in historical times were governed by ancient, undisputed beliefs and customs. One of these tenets was that a woman was the core of a family, regardless of its size. In many cases relatives lived together in a group that was comprised of a woman and her husband, her mother and father, her daughters, her daughters' husbands and any children, grandparents, and other relations who happened to be around. The Apache woman at the center was the hub around which all events, functions, and people revolved smoothly, but occasionally the situation became awkward because of taboos like mother-in-law avoidance.

A man's mother-in-law practically owned him from the day of the wedding. She could order him around like a servant, but she had to dictate her instructions or convey her wishes through her daughter or others in the household. She could not speak directly to him, not even to ask him to chop wood, hunt meat, or drive her somewhere. On the other hand, tradition dictated that to show respect, a son-in-law should never lay eyes on his mother-in-law after the wedding day. Actually, each was obligated not to look at the other, although the avoidance onus fell on the man. The prohibition was still observed so strictly in the late 1940s that a rope was strung down the aisle from front to back at the Mescalero Apache Reservation's Dutch Reformed church. Draped over the rope were curtain-like cloths separating families in order to honor the cultural tradition.

One Chiricahua family who purchased a car in the 1940s strung a clothesline behind the driver's and passenger's seat. They draped blankets over this line from one side of the vehicle to another whenever the man's mother-in-law needed a ride to the center of the reservation, where the agency buildings were located, or to the tribal store to purchase food.

In times past, acquiring food was not as easy for the Apaches and everyone else as it is today. Although farming was not one of the Chiricahuas' routine activities, there were occasions when women worked the land and were responsible for planting, irrigating, harvesting crops and then cooking for the extended family. Corn was a preferred food, and women prepared it in at least two favorite ways: roasting ears with the husks on, or grinding corn into coarse meal, then mixing it with water to make a batter. Responsible for providing drinks for the family as well, certain Apache women made *tiswin*, a favorite alcoholic beverage, for adults. To begin the process, women soaked corn kernels and allowed them to sprout and dry, after which they ground them on a *metate*. Several weeds, roots, and water were then added. They placed the mixture in a large vessel and boiled it for several hours. Next the liquid was poured off and saved, the residue recrushed on the *metate*, added to the liquid, and boiled again. After all this, the women set the blend aside to ferment for twenty-four hours; then it was ready to drink.

Women prepared meals over an open fire and those family members who did not like to eat on separate plates ate from a common dish, sometimes using their fingers or crude, hand-made utensils. Tradition called for an Apache woman to wait until her husband had eaten before she finished what he left; she ate no more than his leftovers.[1] Although their varied roles in family life were pivotal, and the society has been classified as "matrilineal" and "matrilocal," Apache women were subordinate to their men in many situations. Drinking, dancing, and gambling—rare pursuits in days of old—were the exceptions. During these particular exploits, women were men's equals, but life eventually returned to normal, and women resumed their familiar inferior positions and duties.

While traveling the countryside during the seasons with the tribe, a wife carried water for the family in a large watertight bottle, handwoven by her from grasses and reeds she had gathered. Potterymaking, a craft practiced by women in other native groups, was out of the question for the Apaches. The Chiricahua lifestyle was nomadic and therefore unlike the sedentary societies in which breakable pots were used. Consequently, most Apache women were expert basketmakers, using only two techniques—twining and coiling. Twined baskets could be made watertight and were created from squawberry (also used to make a medicinal drink), sumac, and mulberry. In twining, two or more active elements pass over one or two passive elements, the active going before and behind the stiff warp element, and over and under each other alternately so that they "twine" about the warp and, at the same time, about one another.

Practically all coiling is done in a counterclockwise direction and is employed to produce bowls, baskets, and other flat objects. Coiled baskets are comprised almost exclusively of willow, yucca, and cottonwood, with designs in black from the plant known as devil's claw. To begin weaving, a woman selects the amount of sewing splints and foundation rods, together with the devil's claw for working the designs. She soaks the rods and splints in water to make them soft and pliable. Sometimes they are buried in wet soil and drawn out one at a time as needed. As the coiling goes round and round, each spiral increases in size and new rods are added as the first ones are covered. The basket is finished with plain, over and over sewing, but in the twined water jars, some false braiding may be used. Some rims are sewed entirely with devil's claw; others are made with alternating stitches of black and white or with alternating sections.[2] Tu Moonwalker, a premier San Carlos/White Mountain Apache basketmaker of today, uses eight coiling stitches per inch. "When I line [the jar] with pitch," she told me, "it's watertight. Just what the Apaches needed to carry their water in the desert and the mountains."[3]

Living in those environmental conditions and moving about only on foot (before contact with horses) in a never-ending search for food, the Apaches were always challenged by thorny cacti, falling rocks, varmint bites, and confrontations with wild animals. Because of these unavoidable hazards that were associated with day-to-day living, it is fair to assume that injuries occurred frequently and that a goodly portion of those hurts were medicated by the women, who were expected to have considerable knowledge of curing with nature's medicines. For example, the freely growing mescal plant[4] was also used to control bleeding from wounds. Chewing softened the mescal, leaving nothing but the woody fibers remaining. A woman rolled the fibers into a ball and plugged the wound. When hemorrhaging ceased, she removed the plug and inserted more chewed mescal deeper into the path of the wound. Over and over again she chewed and inserted until the wound was under her control and the individual was able to continue moving. If a broken bone had to be set, an Apache woman created a splint from *sotol* cactus slats and, after immobilization, the bone and slats were wrapped with buckskin or rawhide strips. To treat mundane maladies, she smashed the leaves from one variety of the mesquite plant that clustered in dense thickets near an arroyo, and placed the leaves directly on minor lesions such as scrapes, scratches, and some insect bites. As was the case with many other plants, mesquite served several purposes. The plant's beans could be ground into meal for food, and drinking a solution made from the roots boiled in water treated nervousness and colic; a fluid from the leaves served as an eyewash. The inner bark of the mesquite plant was so soft that it was used as diapers for babies in cradleboards.

When more serious afflictions occurred, such as those from contact with snakes, scorpions, tarantulas, giant centipedes, or other poisonous creatures,[5] Apache women treated the wound by first killing the offending creature and then carving out a piece of its body to apply directly on the bite. The next best medicine was placing live crickets, lizards, and spiders on the injury.

To help avoid the ordinary accidents that caused cuts, scratches, bruises, sprains, and strains that were part of desert dwelling, Chiricahuas crafted their hide boots with an upturned toe. The boots were tall, thigh-high, and could be rolled down over and over, making flaps and pockets in which men and women carried necessary items including an awl for crafting new boot soles. It was not unusual for a woman to pack a small stem of sage (*Salvia,* spp.) and other herbs inside the roll of her boot. Sage was thought to be powerful enough to prevent an adult from being hit by lightning.[6]

Apache women knew that routine aches and pains at the campsite or when traveling were helped by drinking a tea made from snakebroom, also called Escoba de Vibora (*Gutierrezia,* spp.), a prolific, many-stemmed plant with yellow flower clusters growing most everywhere in Apacheria.[7] For a sore mouth, possibly the result of chewing bark and berries, women squeezed juice from leaves and stems of the milkweed plant and mixed a very small amount of the liquid with secretions from pine and cottonwood trees to make a mouth-soothing chewing gum. Wild mint steeped in water eased a sore throat that might have resulted from yelling. To reduce fever, women cooked willow and quaking aspen leaves in water and drank it as a tea.

However, regardless of her skills and expertise, an Apache woman did not expect to be complimented by her husband for jobs well done.

Apache men could be distant, aloof, reticent, and the relationship between the sexes was sometimes combative. Men periodically beat their wives, but "not without reason," according to what one informant told author Opler. "If he finds out that she is unfaithful, he whips her, cuts her nose, or else kills her. He would have to have evidence of unfaithfulness and not hearsay, however. Treatment like this does not come for little things. For not obeying him, or for not working, a man would merely scold his wife, and he would do so in private. If the woman has committed adultery, the people think that what happens to her is her own fault and don't say anything about the punishment she gets."[8] The informant referenced a serious situation that obligated the husband "to vindicate the family honor by cutting off the end of his wife's nose."[9] If he did not, he lost face among his peers, which was one of the worst humiliations an Apache could experience.

However, if the husband were caught committing adultery, his wife could only scold him and complain to her relatives about his behavior. Opler's informant told him, "The women don't have power to do too much to the men. A very mean woman might stab her husband at night or something like that. The people wouldn't blame her much, because it is the husband's fault. But only a very hard-up man would marry the woman after this; so that keeps women from killing their husbands."[10]

Violence between Apache men and women has unfortunately come forward in time, occasionally resulting in death. In 1948, Bureau of Indian Affairs teacher Robert S. Ove lived among the Chiricahuas at Whitetail, a separate settlement on the Mescalero Apache Reservation. Along with teaching, he often served as a peacekeeper. One evening the wife of a young man came to Ove's home and complained about her husband's threatening to shoot her. At that time, Ove soothed the volatile situation, but years later, the husband slit her throat, ear to ear. She bled to death and he went to prison for murder.[11]

Chiricahua women were not always the victims of ongoing marital discord, however. Author Morris Opler believed that women were well aware of their rights and did not accept abuse passively. He cited a tale told to him by a Chiricahua. "Not long ago this man started beating up on his wife. She just took him and rolled him under the bed. You know he is paralyzed on one side and is pretty near helpless when you get him like that. It was a low bed and he got stuck there. He stayed there until another fellow came along and let him out. He was there calling to his wife to get him out."[12]

When an Apache woman had had enough of physical violence, cultural customs allowed her to divorce her man, for that reason and for others like infidelity, laziness, impotence, excessive gambling, or sterility. It was easy; she simply put his belongings outside their home. In that case the husband packed his possessions, went back to his mother and began looking for another wife. If the husband was the partner seeking the permanent separation, he told his wife he was going hunting and then never returned. The children of this divorce usually stayed in the mother's camp unless she and her immediate family could not support them. In that case they were given to a female relative of the mother, who had her own home.

Because having multiple wives simultaneously was culturally endorsed, Apache women could share their men, thus reducing the incidence of physical or mental abuse. Life was usually easier under polygamous circumstances, particularly if the wives liked each other, divided the household work fairly and everyone accepted the pecking order that established the first wife as being in charge of the entire household. As a prisoner of war, Geronimo and both his wives occupied a two-room log cabin at Fort Sill, Oklahoma. Wife Zi-yeh and daughter Eva and son Fenton slept in one room while Ih-tedda and daughter Lenna occupied the other room. [Geronimo's biographer, Angie Debo, has identified nine women whom Geronimo married, not all at once, of course.[13]] One or both of those women were of immeasurable help to Geronimo in his garden where year after year he grew cantaloupes and watermelons. And, you can bet that Geronimo did not harvest them himself, nor did he perform any routine household chores—not with two women around.

Building temporary family shelters known as wickiups was also a woman's job in days of freedom. According to information obtained in 1939 by the Federal Writers Project in Arizona, this type of construction required a "circle of poles, juniper, mesquite, pine, whichever grows close by." These poles were set a few inches into the ground at about one-foot intervals and then, "The tops are drawn together and securely lashed [with yucca leaf strands], completing a conical framework," usually seven feet high at the center and eight feet in diameter. This was covered with long grass or pine boughs. An opening at the top center allowed smoke from a central inside fireplace to escape. By their nature wickiups were not permanent structures and were left behind whenever the freely roaming Apaches moved. The Chiricahuas' talent for constructing covers with natural materials shows itself today in the careful way the cooking arbors at the puberty ceremony are built. Built by the reservation's firefighters—who are called Apache Hot Shots— leafy limbs and boughs form the walls and high ceilings of an outdoor room that is rainproof and at least five to ten degrees cooler than the dance grounds just outside. Apaches who choose to live at the puberty ceremony site for four days may also construct their temporary living quarters with the same natural materials and cover their lodgings with bright blue tarps. Fires for cooking inside these quarters are watched carefully, particularly during dry spells.

In historical times, women roamed miles on foot to find and haul firewood for cooking and for warmth, frequently bringing back bulky, heavy bundles of wood on their backs. Before leaving camp, a woman made a "rope" out of rawhide, about five yards long. If the search was successful, she wrapped the brush and sticks she gathered with the tie at either end, leaving a loop in between. To lug the bundle back to camp, she fixed the loop over her forehead, giving balance to the load of wood on her back. To keep it out of the rare inclement weather, she might have placed her bundle under an arbor she constructed at the campsite. When rain was expected, she pulled enough wood inside the wickiup to keep her family dry and warm. In rainy yet warm weather the smoke hole at the top of the wickiup could be covered with hide, which also was used to cover the doorway.

The interior floor of the wickiup was lined with brush and grass that could be removed and replaced when they were dried out or when an Apache woman swept the earthen floor with a broom made of grasses or leafy branches. For sleeping, robes were spread over the floor covering.

Along with looking for wood, women were also obligated to scour the area around a camp for foodstuffs such as walnuts, acorns, piñon nuts, and juniper berries that supplemented the wild game brought to the camp by hunters. Never wandering alone, women traveled in groups of up to six, stopping periodically to drink water from a jug woven by one of them. Wild potatoes, wild onions, and the fruits of the saguaro cactus were available in season. A favorite was the white flowers of the narrow-leaf yucca *(Yucca angustissima)*. The petals were gathered, taken back to camp, and boiled with meat or bones for flavoring. Also, their stems were roasted until soft, then peeled and eaten. Mesquite and other wild beans were plentiful and sweet in the autumn.

Mesquite beans, in particular, were easy to find. They appeared first in spring as long, empty green pods hanging from the trees. As the months progressed, the pods changed color, became pale beige and hung heavily in clusters on the ubiquitous mesquite trees in Apacheria. In late July the pods started to bulge with beans and some species turned red. By September or early October they were ready to be harvested. After pulling the pods off the trees and carrying them back to camp, women split open the pods, removed the beans, and crushed them into a mealy substance that could be mixed with other ingredients to form a thick, tasty, and filling paste. Because they were so plentiful, mesquite beans were a staple of the Apache diet.

If women lived far from a place where mescal was found, they traveled to the spot, established a temporary camp and baked the agave onsite in a pit. Men occasionally accompanied the women and dug the pit, about three feet deep and as long as seven feet or more. Women lined this basin with rocks and wood, prayed over it, and set it afire. When the wood burned down to ashes, they placed the heart of the mescal in the pit, covered it with wet grass and dirt, and allowed it to bake. Smaller plants were ready to be removed within twenty-four hours; larger agaves were ready in two to four days. When the roasted mescal cooled, the woman either carried it herself or tied the plant onto a horse for transportation back to the camp, where its uses were multiple.[14]

One of the Apaches' favorite foods was mescal pudding, a tasty but stringy dish. The mescal fibers are indigestible and after chewing off the sweetness, one simply spits out the remainder. Years ago when I had my first taste of mescal pudding, I was not told how to eat it and chewed and chewed, wondering why in the world the substance did not reduce enough to swallow. At that time I was with the great-granddaughter of Cochise and did not want to insult her by spitting into my handkerchief, but I did not know what else to do. I kept grinding away until out of the corner of my eye I saw her starting to giggle. I had no doubt that I was the cause of her amusement. When she recovered herself, she showed me how to take the strings out of my mouth and throw them on the ground. By the way, these are the same fibers that Apache women plug into wounds to control bleeding.

Some Apache women, such as the wife of a chief or other important person, were exempt from these and other routine household duties. Those wives were expected to take a leadership position, to exercise quite a bit of authority within the group, and to set good examples for other women to follow. Marital status and an excellent reputation permitted a leader's wife to speak at war dances and chiefs' councils, so she was expected to study an issue, formulate her opinions, discuss them with her husband, and then present them in public. Often her duties included catering for special events.

Ishton, the wife of Chief Juh of the Nedni Apaches and the "sister" of Geronimo,[15] was known for her ability to plan, direct, and prepare a victory feast for warriors returning from a raid. She and Geronimo were extremely close, and he was most fond of her. When she labored for days unsuccessfully in childbirth, Geronimo risked his life to be with her. Seeing how close to death she was, as a medicine man he went to a high place and prayed to *Ussen* that her trial be ended and that her life be spared. Back at her side, he saw his prayer answered with the subsequent birth of his nephew, Ishton's son Asa Daklugie. Many years later Daklugie told author Eve Ball about his mother's role in a feast that welcomed warriors back from a raid. Said Asa, "Dressed in her gorgeous beaded buckskin robes, Ishton directed preparations for the feast. Her slaves spread skins and blankets in a semicircle for Juh and his men . . . Cooking pots were placed around the big central fire of logs, and meat was laid to roast on small beds of coals. Jugs of water and *tiswin* were in readiness for the feast. The singers and drummers were to file in and take their places, and the warriors were to follow. But not until my mother signaled did Juh, [dressed] in his best finery, lead the way. After my father had blown smoke in each of the four directions, he raised his arm and the women began serving the food. Roasted venison, mescal, sweet acorn meal cakes and honey were provided,"[16] all under Ishton's able direction and supervision.

Although Ishton decorated her buckskin clothing with beads, most Chiricahua Apache women wore the hides without adornment after tanning and coloring the skin dark brown with the juice of walnuts. Tanning was an incredibly slow undertaking that began with the removal of the hide from an animal, one of the tasks relegated to women. They soaked the hide and then staked it to the ground before the laborious tanning chore started. Bones or stones were favorite implements because they were easily held in one hand. Patiently, forcefully, on their knees and bent over for hours at a time, the women scraped the fur off the hide, inch by inch, to the accompaniment of a nauseating odor and hundreds of flies. Mildred Cleghorn told me, "I have only tanned one buckskin, and that was my first and last. At Whitetail on the Mescalero Apache Reservation in New Mexico, my aunt Gertrude Smith was tanning and I said I wanted to help, so she let me. When you start you can't stop. You have to keep going. If you want to have a nice soft hide, you can't let it get dry. You have to work it dry. That's the old way. I haven't tanned or seen anyone tan hides for years, so I don't know if anyone still does it the old way today. It's hard work, but I know they have all kinds of new soaps now that cut down the time. Good riddance to the hand tanning, but if you could get the same quality of tanning in a modern version that was done by hand, it would be wonderful. The old tanning way took both sides of the skin into consideration, and it produced very soft leather. On the hides I have seen commercially tanned today, only one side is usable for what we want. Commercially tanned hides are not the same."[17]

The tanned material was sewed with sinew that had been removed by a hunter-husband from an animal's loin, preferably a deer. First the woman used an awl[18] made from the sharpened leg bone of the deer to punch holes in the skin. Then she threaded the sinew through the holes and began to create her outfit. A short hide skirt was always tied at the waist and fringed at the knees. The top was usually a fringed, blouse-like garment that dropped down to the waist and covered the breast and back. An Apache woman's personal appearance was important, particularly her hair, which was often tied in the shape of a chestnut, and usually wrapped in chamois or beaver skin.[19] Ever conscious of her image, her appearance was particularly important to her during pregnancy, a condition that was also governed by time-honored do's and don'ts that influenced the behavior of the mother-to-be.

CHAPTER 3

Lifestyles

The main purpose of an Apache marriage in historical times was to produce children who would take the tribe into the future. If pregnancy among newly marrieds did not occur within a reasonable time, cultural assumptions declared that the husband might have been bewitched, or tricked into impotence by a human version of a coyote, or that a wife's sterility could be from adverse circumstances that occurred back during her puberty ceremony. In these situations, Apache medicine men and medicine women were called upon by the husband and wife to alleviate or eliminate these conditions and thus facilitate pregnancy.[1]

Pregnancy was a time of "equanimity, of care without dread, work without exertion, and receiving special attention without becoming spoiled."[2] As in other periods of their lives, women observed certain customs during the pregnancy: they did not ride horses, lift heavy objects, or do anything that could shock the fetus. They did not eat fatty meat, piñon nuts, or intestines. They did not witness ceremonies at which the *Gah'e* danced because the sight of them might scare the baby. They did not argue with outsiders, because they were not certain who was a witch and who was not, and the baby could be hexed if a pregnant woman quarreled with a witch. They did not take long walks, and they did not sit up for long periods of time. They often wore a maternity belt made of the skins of white-tailed and black-tailed deer, mountain lion, and antelope. These animals gave birth without difficulty, and an Apache woman believed that if she wore this belt for a few days only, she would be able to imitate the animals and have an easy birth.

When labor began, a woman was attended by her mother, her

mother's sisters and several other women from the group. If labor was difficult, a medicine man or medicine woman could have been asked to attend. Customs dictated that a woman in labor kneel with her legs apart in front of an oak post, which she used to steady herself. To speed birth, she swallowed four small, light-colored pieces of the inner leaves of the narrow-leaf yucca with salt, one after the other. A midwife, who was often a female relative, massaged her belly downward and bathed her genitals in water in which the crushed root of *Eriogonum jamesii*[3] had been placed. Immediately after the infant was successfully delivered, the midwife cut the cord with a long piece of black flint or the sharp edge of a yucca leaf. If the newborn appeared sluggish, the midwife poured cold water on the baby to shock the infant into life. Also right after birth, the midwife squirted a mixture of her own saliva and warm water over a newborn's body. The baby was then dried and sacred pollen sprinkled on its body.

These traditional customs involving a baby were observed during peaceful times when the Chiricahuas were not being pursued by their enemies. On other occasions, when a woman began labor she put the welfare of the tribe first, often urging them to continue escaping while she remained behind, alone or with a female companion, to give birth. Survival of mother and newborn under those conditions was often just a matter of luck. If they could rejoin their group at some future time, ceremonies for the baby were held later, when safety was assured. If found by the pursuers, the woman and child were either taken as captives or killed.

Disposal of the placenta was also according to custom. Placed in a piece of cloth or blanket, it was deposited in the branches of a nearby fruit-bearing bush or tree. This precious bundle was blessed by the midwife who recited a small prayer at the site, such as "May the child live and grow up to see you bear fruit many times." The family forever considered that place to be sacred, and the parents and child might return there many times in the child's life. Legend has it that Geronimo went back on several occasions as an adult to the place of his birth to lie on the ground and roll over and over toward the four directions in acknowledgment and respect. [Burial of the placenta was out of the question because animals could dig it up and thus, the culture teaches, cause harm to come to the child.]

A baby was usually named during a ceremony that was held immediately after delivery or, depending on the circumstances, could be postponed. The name given to an infant at birth is often not permanent and may change several times during an individual's lifetime. For example, a woman may have been skilled, as a child of nine or ten years, in making dolls, and consequently her birth name would be changed then to reflect that attribute. As she grew into adulthood, she might have been exceptionally generous, so the childhood name would be changed to one that told the world how giving she was. By her senior years she might have gained a reputation as a kindly grandmother and would then take on another name that identified her as such.[4]

A special ceremony was held when the child was about one month old, before being placed in a cradleboard. The infant was first marked with cattail pollen and then the carrier was lifted by a medicine man or medicine woman to the four directions with the baby inside if it was a boy; if a girl, an empty cradle was lifted on high. Amid prayers, the cradle was faced toward the east and after three ritual thrusts, the baby girl was finally placed inside. As an infant matured, charms were sewn onto the slats to protect the child. Opler lists "the right paw of the badger with grass substituted for the bone . . . to protect the child from fright . . . Hummingbird claws and pieces of wildcat skin also act as cradle charms. To ward off colds and other sickness, a length of cholla wood is often tied on the cradle. When anything is wrong with the child, a growth found on the creosote bush is suspended from the canopy."[5]

In many regions of the country, Indian mothers have been keeping and carrying their babies on cradleboards for many centuries. They say it makes the babies feel secure and warm, protects them from harm, and helps their backs grow straight and strong.[6] Each tribe has its own distinctive style of cradleboard and its own customs regarding the construction.

In the Apache way, the unit itself was made four days or more after the birth of the baby. It was not unusual for medicine men or medicine women, at the request of a family, to construct a carrier. They often prepared the materials in advance, sometimes working on the outer frame for a day and then setting it aside, awaiting the moment when they finished crafting the cross pieces and the canopy. Once actual construction began, however, it usually was completed within one day. The cultural assumption was that the medicine man or medicine woman would say the appropriate prayers for the coming child's welfare and long life during each step of creating the cradleboard.

The completed carrier could be toted around on the mother's back, hung on a low tree branch to catch the breeze, or propped against a wall in an upright position so the small occupant could watch the surrounding activity. In cases of very poor families, one cradleboard may be used for all the children or might even be a borrowed carrier. If a baby grew up healthy, other mothers asked to borrow the board for their own babies, hoping that their children would draw strength from the original occupant. The cradleboard had another, sadder use as well. A dead infant could be buried in the cradleboard.

Chiricahua Apache women living at Whitetail on the Mescalero Apache Reservation made cradleboards from natural wood, usually oak, cut from the surrounding forest.[7] Occasionally they used yucca cactus frames, which were bound by buckskin straps and backed with yucca stalks that were split in half and laced with buckskin. Rarely, a length of barbed wire formed the frame's foundation. Each cradle had a strong, slatted back and a curved top like a handle, making it simple and convenient to pick up.

Babies spent quite a bit of time in their cradleboards, being removed in most cases only for nursing. When they grew sleepy they were put back in onto "soft bedding of shredded bark or crumpled grass . . . Over this bedding was laid the tanned, spotted hide of a fawn, the hair side up, or at times the skins of cottontail rabbits. The baby was then placed on this and between its legs for a diaper was put soft, shredded bark. Another fawn skin, hair side in, was laid over it, the edges tucked in about the baby's body and up under its feet. It was then laced into the carrier with a strip of buckskin."[8] A movable piece of wood served as a footrest. As the baby grew, this simple square could be moved downward, allowing room for the baby to stretch its legs.

Chiricahua Apache mothers were naturally concerned about the development of their infants' eyes, which were so important as the child matured. Without good vision an Apache could be in danger from enemies, from snakes, bears, or other dreaded creatures, from thorny cacti, and from all of the obstacles faced daily by desert people. To assist a child's eyes, the mother occasionally hung small items such as feathers, pine cones, a squirrel's tail, beads, or other shiny baubles from the top of the cradleboard. Particularly useful to Chiricahua mothers were pieces of wood that had been hit by lightning—a lucky charm, so to speak—and anything else that could have assured that the child would have a long and healthy life. Turquoise was a special favorite. Today, mothers attach mobiles of birds or other flying creatures on crib rails or hang them from the ceiling to accomplish the same goals.

If the baby in the cradleboard was a boy, the cradleboard "roof" over the child's head identified him as such with four slits carved into the wood. Girls were identified by a full moon or half moon carved into the shady overhang. Buckskin lace tie-ins were placed on the right for a girl, on the left for a boy. Infants remained in cradleboards until they were approximately six or seven months old, when they were allowed to crawl on the ground, under adult supervision.

When an Apache woman rode horses, she kept her baby strapped on her back in a cradleboard. A leather strap or a loop similar to the one used to carry wood encircled the mother's forehead. She balanced the carrier on her back by moving her head, even when the horse was at a full gallop. In the 1950s women wore the strap around their shoulders—probably a sign of changing times and styles.[9]

Ceremonies were culturally prescribed at certain stages of an infant's life. For example, first haircuts were given to youngsters in the spring of any year with a medicine man or woman in attendance. Locks of the child's hair were buried under a fruit tree, insuring a full head of hair. Moccasins were usually placed on an infant's feet before the second birthday, also under the watchful eye of a medicine man or medicine woman who sang sacred songs during this ceremony.

As Chiricahua children developed, they heard stories about the natural environment and all things that grow or walk on it. A favorite animal has always been the coyote, well known as a trickster. However, occasionally the coyote himself is tricked, and that causes great merriment among the listeners. For example, one favorite tale of Apache children relates the trouble between a coyote and a turkey. It seems Coyote saw a turkey high up in some pine trees and got an ax to chop down the tree. Just about the time the tree started to fall, the turkey flew to another tree. Coyote also tried to cut that tree down, but it had a thick base, and so the poor animal chopped all day until he was exhausted. Just as the tree was ready to fall, the turkey flew to the next tree. Coyote went after him and tried to chop that one down too. Poor Coyote finally gave up because he was worn out.[10]

In storytelling sessions Chiricahua children learned all about the moccasin game, one of the most important games of chance in the culture. According to custom, the story of the moccasin game can be told only on a winter night. "If you tell this story in summer," a Chiricahua told

Morris Opler, "you will see bad animals like the rattlesnake."[11] The tale has to do with the time when all the world was in darkness and a fight between birds and animals occurred to win daylight. Birds wanted the brightness but the animals preferred the night. Opposing sides lined up, facing each other, but the animals had an advantage in that a great monster called Giant was on their side. In days of old, sticks were the treasures that had to be won by either the birds or the animals, and the winners had the right to kill the losers. The winners then were rewarded with either daylight or darkness. Giant helped the animals garner more sticks than the birds but when Turkey played for the birds, they began to regain their sticks. Finally, the animals had only a few left and day began to break. A little wren flew in front of the animals and sang "Daybreak is coming! Daybreak is coming!" Giant became angry and took a stick from the fire and pushed the wren away. As the bird flew up on a cliff, the rocks opened a little and daylight streamed through. Then the animals lost the last stick and the birds began killing them. Giant left but could not get away before the birds began shooting at him with bows and arrows. A little lizard shot the giant right on the bottom of his hind foot and the monster fell. As the birds chased the remaining animals, they found a bear in a thicket. He was in such a hurry to get away that he put his moccasins on the wrong feet, which, according to the tale, is why his feet look that way today.[12]

Contemporary Chiricahuas play a version of the old moccasin game that is derived from the mythological battle between the birds and the animals. Sides are chosen, a fire is lit, and each side buries four moccasins in a row with only the tops visible. Songs describing the first confrontation between the birds and the beasts are sung by contestants on either side. A member of one group places a bone in one of the moccasins on his side, and when a blanket—which has been lowered between the two groups—is lifted, someone from the other side attempts to strike the moccasin holding the bone. If he is correct, the bone passes to his side for concealment. If he is incorrect, his group must pay the opposition a certain number of yucca cactus "counters," of which there is only a limited number. When one side has won all the "counters," the game is over. Chiricahuas, who fervently love to gamble, place bets on each stroke of the stick and on the final outcome of the game. Yelling and cheering accompany this game from start to finish—unusual behavior, one could say, from a group of individuals who have a reputation for being reserved. Yet those of us who know the Chiricahuas are familiar with their passions and do not find any expression of emotions out of the ordinary, especially those relating to their children.

Today, as in historical times, most Chiricahua Apaches show great love for their children. While the times have changed, certainly, and contemporary Chiricahuas face obstacles and temptations unimagined by their ancestors, for the most part they try to rear their young children in the spirit of times past. Then physical discipline of children was almost never required, for they were trained to be obedient, and that was done often by simply telling them not to do certain things and expecting compliance. Opler has recorded a number of "don'ts" that were told to him by an informant who remembered his early years. Among these were "Do not use a bad word which you wouldn't like to be used to you; don't steal from your friends; don't laugh at anybody or make fun of anybody; do not take bread or a drink or a piece of meat before the rest start to eat; don't run into another person's camp as though it was your own."[13]

The Apache child was definitely made aware of certain dangers, such as the possible presence of an enemy nearby, and was taught to be very quiet at a command. Some young children were unable to understand the need for silence under those conditions and so a covering was put on their heads until they stopped crying or fussing. I was told a legend about an occasion when the Chiricahuas were in flight from the U.S. Army somewhere in Arizona and three infants would not stop wailing. Geronimo approached the mothers and asked if he could strangle the babies because the continued sounds of crying would reveal the group's position. The mothers agreed. Whether this tale is true cannot now be determined, but it serves as an example of the dire need to have the children cooperate in those days.

When children were guilty of absolutely terrible behavior, of course they were punished. As a young girl, Mildred Cleghorn and her boy cousin played in a barn and accidentally set it on fire. They escaped into her mother's arms who, sometime later when they had calmed down, disciplined the children by putting both of them in gunnysacks. Although she clearly remembered the situation, "I could never get [my mother] to admit she did that, or even say yes or no," Mildred told me. "She just said, 'Oh, I wouldn't do that.'"[14]

Ordinarily, though, Chiricahua parents were usually gentle with their children, even through all the ordinary and extraordinary frustrations encountered in raising them. Child rearing was entirely in the hands of the mother, maternal grandmother, and the mother's sisters, who remained in charge of a girl. At some early point, determined by the men in the family, a little boy was taken in hand by his father, his maternal grandfather, and his mother's unmarried brothers. As soon as he was able, he was taught how to shoot a bow and arrow and was permitted to observe how the men crafted their weapons. He learned how to hunt, participated in a sweat bath, was trained in physical fitness, and engaged in rigorous competition with his peers. Most important, he learned survival techniques. Still later the boy was invited to accompany his father or uncle on a hunt, and after that he was apprenticed to a warrior. As the warrior's "horseholder," the boy gained first-hand experience in the dangers and rewards of the warpath. After a certain number of forays into battle beside his mentor, the boy was considered ready to be on his own under those conditions.

While the boy was absorbing the ways of men, girls remained with their mothers and maternal relatives, learning the ways of women, observing their mother's daily routine and participating in household tasks. A girl was instructed on how to care for the younger children in her family, how to gather wood, and how to bring in water, among other tasks. Girls were also trained in physical activities. They participated in races on foot and on horseback, competing against boys of the same age. Both genders learned how to hunt small game and follow tracks. Boys and girls learned how to use a rifle, a throwing stick, a knife, a slingshot, and bow and arrows. Both were taught combat techniques, including shooting and running, escape and evasion techniques, the use of camouflage, and how to handle horses. Said Michael Darrow, the Fort Sill Apache tribal historian, "The qualifications, like being able to shoot a gun, ride a horse and run far and fast and the other miscellaneous qualities that would apply to male warriors were the same for women. The training process was such that essentially everybody had the same training, but with different emphasis. Everybody was supposed to know how to do everything, whether they do it or not. So, the men would need to know how to cook and sew because there might be an occasion when they would need to do that. Women would need to know how to ride horses and follow tracks. Some women would be particularly skilled at things like following tracks or shooting or running. They wouldn't be discouraged from doing it, but they wouldn't necessarily be encouraged."[15]

By the time the youngsters of both genders were at this junction in their lives, the childhood problems that could have occurred were long gone, as should have been the need for parental discipline. Prior to then, however, both parents usually reprimanded a child, but any close relatives could also scold or punish an unruly boy or girl. Corporal punishment was practically unknown, for the threats issued by the parents, e.g., a clown with a big basket will take them away if they did not behave, frightened the child enough to cause good behavior. The physical problems of childhood, such as bedwetting, were handled not by reprimands but by putting a bird's nest in the bed with the children, then throwing the wet nest to the east right in front of the child. Thoughtless children, as another example, were often sent on wild-goose chases and when they returned were told why. And then there were the stories. Lessons inherent in stories were quite important, for these also taught the characteristics of the land that sustained them, how to honor it and survive on it, games to play, how to whittle a bow and arrows, how to weave baskets, and other culturally relevant information that was necessary for youngsters to know.

Of course, all, if not most of these lessons necessarily came to a halt in 1886 when the Chiricahua Apaches were imprisoned. At a loss over what to do with the 160 Apache children who also became prisoners of war, the United States government contracted with a group of nuns to teach and care for the youngest, while those older were sent to the Carlisle Indian Training School in Pennsylvania.[16] A letter from then–Secretary of the Interior L. Q. C. Lamar to the president pro tempore of the Senate acknowledged receipt of a Senate resolution that stated

By these papers it will be seen that all of the youth among those Indians between the ages of twelve and twenty-two years, numbering, it is believed, 44 Indians in all, have been transferred to and placed under educational and industrial training at the Carlisle Indian Training School in Pennsylvania; and that upon recommendations of the officers of the Army having the custody of the Indians at Fort Marion, provision has been made for educational training of the younger children to the number of 60, by the Sisters of Charity[17] at Saint Augustine, Fla., at the rate of $7.50 per quarter each, as shown by the copy of Contract (herewith) between the Indian Bureau and the Director of the Bureau of Catholic Indian Missions, commencing January 1, 1887 . . . It will be seen by these papers that the latest report in possession of this Department as to the number of these Indians is that of October 1, 1886, when 469 were confined at Fort Marion. Since that date 44 have been removed to Carlisle.[18]

Sister Mary Albert, the community archivist at the Congregation of the Sisters of St. Joseph in St. Augustine, Florida, told me that a young nun, Mother Alypius, of French origin, was in charge of providing educational services to the youngest children at Fort Marion. These were the children who were not sent to Carlisle because they were too young. Instead, they were permitted to remain at the St. Augustine prison site with their parents or other relatives who were caring for them. "Mother Alypius would take the children out of the fort and walk them down the street to the convent, a ten minute walk," she said. "Although the government expected the children to learn only numbers and letters from the nuns, and paid them only to teach children, there was much more. The adult Apaches also became part of the lessons taught at the fort, were very eager to learn and were so impressed with Mother Alypius that when another nun temporarily took her place, the Apache men were very reserved toward the new educator. Because of the tribal concept of respect for authority figures, the Apaches accepted the teachers because they knew the nuns were instructing the children at the request of the United States government.

"The contacts between the nuns and the Apaches were 'wholesome.' There was good humor between the cultures and a good climate of relations among most of the people of St. Augustine and the Apaches. Some people, however, had been through experiences with the Florida Seminole Indians and were more fearful of the Apaches.

"The children used the bath house on the premises of the convent, which was a place to swim and they went into the water under the supervision of the Sisters. When the children were taken into the church, like electricity they jumped from bench to bench, so educating these children was not just a matter of teaching the ABCs. Their mental health was also important. The mingling of children with people from another culture broke down resistance. Because the children were cooped up at the fort, walking to the convent gave them some sense of freedom, as did the interaction between the younger nuns and Apache children."[19]

Until the nuns could ready a facility for the students, "the old folks said one of the casemates was used as a classroom," Mildred Cleghorn said.[20] Instructions in reading, writing, drawing, and singing were conducted daily from nine o'clock in the morning until noon. The Sisters had procured needed school supplies such as books, tablets, and pencils for the pupils to use and brought them to the fort. Unexpectedly, the youngsters' lessons were watched over by the Apache men, who became so interested in the lessons that they too were soon drawing with crayons and singing religious and patriotic songs. While the image of Chiricahua Apache men cooperating so completely may be difficult to understand, it certainly is not impossible, and serves as another example of the adults' regard for and involvement with their children.

Before he was sent to Carlisle, James Kaywaykla was one of the youngsters imprisoned at Fort Marion in St. Augustine. In later years, referring to the Sisters, he said, "I will never forget the kindness of those good women, nor the respect in which we held them. For the first time in my life I saw the interior of a church and . . . realized more fully that not all White Eyes [the Apache nickname for Anglos] were cruel and ruthless, but that there were some among them who were gentle and kind."[21]

The older brothers, sisters, and cousins of these young children were not so fortunate—their experiences with education were much different. The Carlisle School was located far from Florida, in the Cumberland Valley of Pennsylvania, about nineteen miles from Harrisburg, on the grounds of a former Revolutionary Army post. It had been abandoned in the 1870s, after being used for years as a training school for cavalry. In 1879 the buildings were donated to the Department of the Interior for use as an educational establishment for Indians. Carlisle's stated purpose was to "train the Indian youth of both sexes to take upon themselves the duties of citizenship. Indian young men and young women are given thorough academic and industrial training, which prepares them to earn a living, either among their own people or away from the reservation in competition with whites. It is primarily a vocational school for both sexes. Its graduates and ex-students are engaged as efficient workers and leaders among their own people on the reservation, and as teachers and officials in the government service, and are successfully competing with whites, away from the reservation, in the trades and professions."[22]

The first group of 96 Chiricahua children was literally taken from their prisoner-of-war families on October 23, 1886, and shipped to the Pennsylvania school; the figure would have been 100, but four children were unable to travel for unknown reasons. James Kaywaykla told Eve Ball,

"Officers and their wives went through the camp [Fort Marion] and selected children to go to Pennsylvania to school. Part of them went by train, part by sea. I was with the latter and I was the youngest child to go . . . except for the terror of another separation from our people, and the uncertainty of what was to be done with us, we were well treated. Being out of sight of land frightened us, but not more than the bewildering experience of crossing New York City."[23]

Upon arrival at Carlisle, their traditional clothing was discarded, their hair was cut, and they were dropped into a closed community of children from many different tribes, with whom they had no common language, history, or culture. Communication with their parents was impossible. They had to eat strange food, attend English-only classes in the basics of reading, writing, and arithmetic, and learn unfamiliar vocational skills. Boys were taught how to run dairy cows, how to farm, raise hogs, grow plants and work in greenhouses, and how to raise chickens. They could also study baking, blacksmithing, bricklaying and plastering, carpentry and cabinetmaking, carriage trimming and upholstering, harnessmaking, mechanical drawing, painting, photography, plumbing and steamfitting, printing, shoemaking, stationary engineering, tailoring, tinsmithing, and wheelwrighting. Girls could study cooking, housekeeping, laundering, nursing, and sewing. Other subjects offered children of both genders were music, native Indian arts such as weaving, beadwork, copper and silversmithing, along with physical culture, and something called telegraphy.

In the summers the students were sent away from the school to local farms for "hands-on" experience. Known as the "outing program," this newfound knowledge of how the larger society functioned was designed to raise the children's self-esteem and accustom them to put into practice those skills they had learned in the classroom[24] and by so doing, "promote the assimilationist goals of the federal government."[25]

Adding to the children's miseries, contagious diseases dramatically affected their strengths and abilities. Vulnerable to most ailments, some became immediately ill upon arrival in Pennsylvania. Along with getting sick from close contact with other ailing Native American students at the school, the outing system continued to expose Chiricahua youngsters to diseases against which they had no immunity.[26] In too many cases, the children became terminally ill. When deaths were so many that they became an embarrassment to the superintendent of the school and raised the government's concern, a compromise was reached. Those children for whom there was no hope of recovery were put on trains and sent back to the prison camp to die among their families. Some did not live that long and perished on the train. Their corpses were lifted off the train by fellow students and placed gently in the arms of heartbroken parents. By shipping ailing students back home, the school's death rate was not so dramatic and public attention, via newspaper reports, was kept at a minimum. Chappo Geronimo, son of the warrior, avoided being a statistic. Sent home from Carlisle when he was near death, he died from tuberculosis three days after arriving at the prison camp in Mount Vernon, Alabama.

Within one year, more than fifteen of the children had died from tuberculosis, and within another year the total had risen to at least twenty-seven. "The school ought not to bear this affliction any longer," wrote a distressed Superintendent Pratt on May 24, 1889. "Quite a considerable proportion of those who remain are drifting downward. We should either be relieved at once of the care of the whole party or they should be thoroughly sifted and those in precarious health sent to their people . . . They have no home, no country, no future, and life has become hardly worth living. I hope that at the earliest practicable date something may be arranged covering the disposition of the whole party. If thoroughly sifted and the unhealthy disposed of, there is no possible objection to the others . . . It is important that we make immediately a change for seven of the girls. Two, or it may be three, will take [to] their beds next week and we may be compelled to bury them here . . . I respectfully request your authority to send seven of these Apaches at once to Mt. Vernon Barracks under the care of one of my teachers, using $117.89 toward paying the expenses and the balance I will pay from my Charity Fund. This action will ease the situation until a conclusion in regard to the whole number is reached."[27]

In April, 1887, twelve married men and one bachelor living with their families at Fort Marion were ordered to Carlisle. These future students traveled by train from Fort Marion to the seaport town of Fernandia, and from there to Charleston, South Carolina. They sailed to New York and then traveled by horse-drawn cabs to the tip of Manhattan Island where a ferry took them across the Hudson River to Jersey City, New Jersey. The last segment of the trip was by train from New Jersey through Philadelphia to Carlisle, Pennsylvania.

The lives of those children, healthy or sick, who survived their educational experience at Carlisle, were abruptly redirected in a manner far, far from tradition and familiarity. No more would the boys leap among boulders shooting their homemade, whittled bows and arrows at each other or at the jackrabbits dashing out of their paths. No more could they be apprentices to the warriors and glory in holding horses at the ready for their mentors. No more would they race their ponies across the Arizona desert. No more would the girls make dolls out of cottonwood roots and dress them in hide skirts. No more could they pick herbs with their mothers and learn their uses. No more would they comb their mothers' beautiful long black hair with cactus thorns. And the puberty ceremony—the one ritual that meant so much to the girls—was suddenly now a thing of the past, existing only in their memories.

CHAPTER 4

The Puberty Ceremony

What is the puberty ceremony and why is it so important? Along with the fact that it was decreed by White Painted Woman, author Opler saw it as "a prayer to the forces . . . that they grant the young Chiricahua girl health and vigor."[1] It was and still is a rite that publicly marks the passage of a girl from her youth to early adulthood. In historical times, the ritual also demonstrated for all to see the character of the girl's family, especially that they successfully brought her to this special crossroads of her life. Significantly, the ceremony announced that the maiden was approaching marriageable age and that she came from a strong family of wealth, power, and importance.

Women members of a girl's family could predict with some certainty when she would start to menstruate and then preparations for the ritual began. The girl's parents and female relatives started to store various ceremonial items such as a drinking tube, scratcher, buckskin, eagle feathers, and a deer hoof rattle. Foods considered to be rare delicacies were gathered: piñon nuts, mesquite beans, and yucca. The buckskin to be used for her dress was cut into two pieces, usually by a female relative, who decorated it heavily with beads and fringe, at the end of which were tied tiny tin bells, often made from the metal lids of cans confiscated from the Apaches' enemies. Throughout this period, which lasted about one year, the girl took lessons in the meaning and processes of the ceremony from an elder, often a medicine man or medicine woman.

Finally the exciting time arrived. At dawn of the first day of the ceremony, a sponsor [often a female family friend akin to a "godmother"] bathed the girl, washed her hair with the suds of the yucca root and left it flowing down her back. The sponsor dressed the girl as she faced east inside a special tipi erected just for her. Older Apache women, gathered around her, prayed as each article of clothing was placed on the maiden's body. Two feathers from the tail of a female eagle were tied to the hair over the crown of her head. Strings of pieces of shell, if available, and necklaces of black and white beads [Chiricahua women's colors] were placed around her neck. To assure that she would have a good appetite throughout her life, she ate a piece of wild fruit marked with pollen from the cattail reed. The older woman attached a length of the same reed and a wooden scratcher to her dress. Throughout the four-day ceremony the maiden used the scratcher for an itch rather than her fingernails. Chiricahuas believe that if the maiden comes in contact with water, it will invite rain which, naturally, would ruin the outdoor ceremony, so the girl drank water through a reed. Her sponsor told her that any unpleasant character traits exhibited by her during the ceremony would distinguish her for the rest of her life. For example, if she indulged in excessive laughter, she would have a prematurely wrinkled face. Her sponsor admonished her not to lose her temper, not make fun of the unfortunate, and not to use harsh language. On the brighter side, she was told she was allowed to talk [but only a little], had to listen to what was told to her, and always had to maintain her dignity.

When a select group of Apache men finished digging a fire pit and raising a ceremonial tipi over it on the sacred grounds on the first morning of the ritual, the girl and her attendants left her tipi and strolled across the grounds. The attendants arranged a buckskin on the ground in front of the ceremonial tipi and the girl knelt on it. As a blessing, the sponsors marked her face with sacred pollen from a small buckskin bag after lifting the pollen to the four directions. Then the sponsor marked her right shoulder, left shoulder, chest, back, and swiped the pollen across her nose. The girl repeated this process on her attendant and all who wished to be painted by her.

The maiden then dropped face down on the buckskin and was rubbed from foot to head, right side to left by her sponsor. This hands-on approach ensured that she would have a good disposition, good morals, and good health that would result in a long life and many children.[2]

Next in the ceremony the attendants traced four footprints on the buckskin with pollen and the girl fit her feet into the outlines. Symbolically, this indicated that she would always walk with the sacred pollen and that her way would be healthy and lucky.

A medicine man placed a basket tray containing ritual objects about thirty paces to the east of the ceremonial tipi. When the appropriate time in the puberty ceremony approached, the sponsor pushed the girl out to run. She hurried down to the basket, circled it, and headed back to the tipi. By so doing, she imitated White Painted Woman, running to the east and returning as a beautiful, ageless woman. Each time she returned, the basket was brought closer to the tipi so that after four runs, the girl was finished. Her posture as she ran was believed to symbolize physical fitness, a trait that was sorely desired when the Chiricahua Apaches were evading their enemies. After this symbolic run, the maiden went back to her tipi to rest until evening.

After dark the girl came to the ceremonial tipi where medicine men sang in low voices and shook deer hoof rattles while she danced to the songs. This part of the ritual continued until midnight or thereabouts of the first, second, and third nights with little change except for an occasional rest period. Seated inside the tipi around a fire in the central fire pit were the girl's sponsor and female relatives.

A special ceremony concluded the puberty ceremony on the fifth morning. Medicine men began the closing rites by painting an outline of a sun on the palms of their left hands just as the sun entered the tipi. Then they rubbed this over the head and face of the girl who was subsequently painted with white clay inside the tipi. She was then led out into the sunlight and the ceremony was over.[3]

When sponsoring this ancient ritual in historical times, a family provided food and entertainment for everyone who chose to come to the four-day celebration. Today, the basic premise remains the same, but there are some differences. For example, it has become very costly for a girl's parents to feed all the attendees, sometimes one hundred or more, three meals a day for the full four days. Consequently, *all* family members, including the extended family, may be called upon to share the expense. The cost, sometimes as high as $10,000, includes the wages paid to a woman who acts as the maiden's godmother before, during, and after the ceremony and payment to the medicine men and medicine women who are an integral part of the occasion. Another woman who gets paid for her essential services organizes the food preparation, supervises the workers she has called upon for help, and directs the men who build the cooking fires and move the cast-iron buckets of hot lard [for fry bread] onto and off the fires. If no men are around, women family members pitch in and do the hard work, and everything else related to the occasion, including serving food to dozens of hungry and thirsty people morning, noon, and night.

Breakfasts of boiled meat, potatoes, chili and beans, a traditional pudding, coffee and cold drinks are served on the sacred dance ground in large containers each morning. Because everyone is hungry, especially on the first morning at the conclusion of the opening ceremony itself, the food disappears quickly and more of this and that is continually brought from the cooking arbor that has been specifically reserved for the maiden and her family.

At lunch and dinner, lines begin forming outside the cooking arbor as soon as rough-hewn wooden tables are set up in front of the several entrances. One by one, the women bring large pots of food to the table, servers take their places behind the food and prepare to serve chili and beans, boiled meat, potato salad, corn, fry bread, and the mescal pudding. Paper plates, plastic utensils, and napkins occupy one end of the table and a tall container full of coffee, soda, or a sugary drink sits at the other end surrounded by paper cups. There is no such thing as "running out of food"—family members and their employees make certain of that.

One year I participated in a puberty ceremony conducted for the daughter of a friend. The young woman was older, at age seventeen, than most of the girls that year but she wanted a ceremony nonetheless. "I think she's too old," an elder remarked to me, and that would have been true a century ago, but no longer. As years have gone by, some of the "rules" have been stretched, including what comprises the contents of the "giveaway" that occurs at the end of the first morning's ceremony. While once fruits and nuts were distributed among the attendees, today balloons, bubble gum, lollipops, candy, boxes of Cracker Jacks, and the old standbys of fruit and nuts are thrown from the backs of pickup trucks driven onto the sacred grounds for that purpose. At Mescalero, Mildred Cleghorn would always rush into the crowd of youngsters who were yelling and waving their arms at men standing in the beds of trucks and throwing goodies. She inevitably returned, a big smile on her face, to her friends and relatives with pockets full of sweets and crunchies that she shared.

Years ago a Chiricahua man told me that his grandfather said that when the people were still free but running from the United States Army and a girl came of age, they stopped their flight and held a puberty ceremony, albeit sometimes shortened in duration, depending on the degree of danger. Regardless of how many times this delay happened, they were never found or captured by the military as they conducted the ceremony. Once though, they got away just in time. Asa Daklugie told Eve Ball of an occasion when the people "knew the Cavalry was after them, but when one of the mothers announced that her daughter had reached maturity, the band had to observe the puberty rite. Women were baking mescal when we were attacked from the north and west. Unknown to us, another troop . . . was coming in from the east to cut us off from Mexico. We had a terrible time there in order to cover the flight of the women."[4]

My job during one ceremony was to make the fry bread in the traditional Chiricahua way—over a pit fire in the cooking arbor standing in front of a large, black, bubbling cauldron of liquid lard. In my hands I held a lightweight, long, tree limb with short, forked branches on one end. Apache women sitting on a low wooden bench behind me patted dough in their hands, forming a circle with it, making it ready to be stuck onto a fork of the branch when I swung the limb around. Poised as far away from the heat as I could get, I then dropped the raw dough into the boiling liquid, watched it for a few seconds and quickly turned it over by stabbing it with one of the limb's forks and executing what could be called a flip without splashing the lard. The object is to fry the dough sufficiently but not too much, lest it turn brown and be crusty, and therefore inedible, according to Chiricahua custom. When the bread swimming in the lard was finished, I speared it, raised it, allowed it to drip for a few seconds and then carefully placed it in a basket lined with a red bandanna. Other Apache women, standing ready, quickly scooped up the basket when it was full, took the bread outside to be served, and then brought the empty basket back to me for refills. From this personal experience I can truthfully say that it is most difficult to stand for an hour or so in front of a blazing fire on a hot July day to make fry bread! When my "turn" was finished, I collapsed into a nearby aluminum patio chair and had a long drink of cold water. Another woman took my place and the cooking continued, for the hungry people in line for food outside the arbor were asking for more and more fry bread.

After the last meal of each day—an early supper—is served during the four-day celebration, all activity comes to a halt. The women who have worked ceaselessly preparing and serving food join others on the sacred dance grounds waiting for darkness. Just before nightfall at Mescalero, burly Apache men begin toting kindling and heavy tree limbs to the center of the outdoor arena while family, friends, and special visitors carry aluminum patio chairs to the setting and place them in a wide circle. A set of permanent bleachers and two sets of temporary bleachers surround the grounds and are filled quickly with strangers, newcomers, and youngsters. Beyond the dance grounds, food concessions line a passageway opposite a small area set aside for arts and crafts vendors.

A man designated as the fire starter walks out of the growing shadows toward the center of the dance arena where other men have placed the wood in the shape of a tipi. The fire starter bends down and lights the kindling at the bottom of the pile. In a short time the fire blazes and a troop of Mountain Spirit Dancers appear on the perimeter of the dance grounds. Very young children "ooh" and "aah" at the sight of the *Gah'e,* and mothers gather the youngsters closely. Some women whisper to their children, others provide laps for the kids. Adult men and women sitting in the wide circle stop visiting with friends and grow silent.

As is customary, these masked dancers approach the bonfire first from the east, swaying from left to right as they near the blaze. They raise their "swords" high with outstretched arms, lower them, make the unusual sound of a "coo," and then back up a few steps. This ritual is carried out four times before the dancers move clockwise to the next direction. When the cardinal points have been respected, the drummers sitting on the west side of the grounds begin their part, and then the dancers circle the fire, performing their indescribable steps for hours on end. The Chiricahuas believe these *Gah'e* represent supernatural beings who have great power similar to that of Child-of-the-Water. While in former times they were believed to keep disease away from the Apaches, they also dance for the girls at the puberty ceremony.

According to mythology, these *Gah'e* were not known before the Great Flood. When the waters receded, there were many, many Indians on earth who were very religious. One camp in particular contained many thousand Chiricahuas but only one man among them knew the *Gah'e* and how to "make" the ceremony. Curious, someone from the camp asked this man what the dancers were all about, what good they were. The man agreed to show the Apaches but warned them that they must not come to the tent where the dancers were going to be painted. If someone broke that rule, danger would be the consequence.

Another tale concerns the protective function of the *Gah'e* back in the time when the Chiricahuas were being chased by the Mexican army.

With weapons such as bows and arrows and spears, the Apaches were no match for the guns of the Mexicans. When they were surrounded, a man and woman slipped out. As they ran, the man prayed to the *Gah'e*. A nearby mountain opened and the *Gah'e* emerged, surrounding the soldiers and driving them into a mountain cave. Then they shut the entryway and none of the soldiers ever returned. This story illustrates one of the protective functions of the *Gah'e*, who, it must be understood, are impersonated by the Mountain Spirit Dancers and are not gods themselves.

These dancers are quite an impressive sight. Naked from the waist up, their arms and upper part of the body are entirely covered with paint, usually black or white or yellow. Designs are painted on the chest and arms of the men in contrasting colors and may be a zigzag line, a stepped line, a four-pointed star or a cross. Their buckskin skirts, full of cone-shaped jingles, are held in place with broad black belts. To fashion the noisemakers, the metal is cut to a proper size, placed over a depression in a board, and struck at the median point. This curls the tin, making it easy to press them together with the fingers to form the cone. The jingle is then attached to the garment on a length of fringe.[5] Their high moccasins have an upturned toe if the dancer is Chiricahua. [At the puberty ceremonies on the Mescalero Apache Reservation not all the dancers are Chiricahuas; Mescalero and Lipan men also dance. The presence or absence of the upturned toe on their moccasins can discern their band affiliations, for only the Chiricahuas wear the upturned toes.] The dancers carry painted wooden sticks in each hand, and long, narrow streamers with eagle feathers attached are tied just above their elbows. A black hood fits over their heads and is gathered at the neck by a drawstring. Two tiny holes for the eyes are the only openings. A tiny piece of abalone shell may be suspended at the forehead.

By far, the most dramatic element of this costume is the uprights attached to the dancers' hoods. Opler describes them as "spreading prongs of a piece of oak which has been split, soaked in water, and heated until it could be worked. At its upper end this piece is connected to the yucca or sotol that rises above it. A bunch of turkey feathers or some green juniper is tied at the point of union. The superstructure of wooden slats looks like a great, squarish candelabra balanced on the top of the dancer's head. It is essentially a horizontal bar to which vertical pieces approximately two feet high have been attached at two ends and in the middle. From each end of the horizontal support hand are two or four short lengths of wood called "earrings." They strike against one another, making a sound that has become a symbol for the approach of the dancers. From the tops of the vertical pieces float downy eagle feathers."[6]

Dancing with the *Gah'e* around the sacred fire is reserved for Apache women only. No men allowed. After the blessing of the fire rituals are concluded, women wrap themselves in their shawls and step onto the dance grounds. Left foot first, they begin a difficult dance step that leads them around the fire and the Mountain Spirit Dancers in a broad circle. Women of all ages may join the dancing circle at any time, or start another. Moving to the sound of the drums and the men singers' voices, the women surround the dancers who, in turn, encircle the fire. It is a magnificent sight and one that has its roots in the ageless instructions of the ancient cultural heroine called White Painted Woman, still alive in the hearts and minds of the Chiricahua Apaches.

Lenna Geronimo wearing a puberty dress.
Courtesy Smithsonian Institution

*Ha-o-zinne, Chiricahua Apache, third wife of Chief Naiche,
Fort Sill, 1898. Courtesy Fort Sill Museum*

◄ *Marianetta, wife of Geronimo.
Courtesy Smithsonian Institution*

Apache Indian woman sitting with one child on knee and other standing, Mount Vernon Barracks. Courtesy U.S. Army Military History Institute

◄ *Amy White (left) and Blossom White, Fort Sill Apache daughters of George Wratten. Courtesy Fort Sill Museum*

Group portrait of an Apache family. Man standing, woman seated with one child on either side of her. Possibly Kaytennae and Guyen; children's identity unknown. Courtesy U.S. Army Military History Institute

46

Two Apache women and two children seated in between rows of board and batten cabins for housing Apaches at Mt. Vernon Barracks in grove of trees. Courtesy U.S. Army Military History Institute

Chiricahua Apache students at the Carlisle School in Pennsylvania, ca. 1890. James Kaywaykla is small boy on floor. Jason Betzinez is back row, center. To his right is Asa Daklugie, the nephew of Geronimo. Courtesy Frisco Native American Museum

Chiricahua Apache children at Fort Sill. Probable identification: Back row, left to right: *Lena Morgan with baby in cradleboard, Lisa Tiss-nol-thos, Hopkins Smith.* Center row: *Eva Morgan, Martin Simmons, Peter Toklanny, Jason Kaywaykla.* Front row: *Willie Gooday, Neshe's daughter, Agnes Chihuahua, Juanita Loco, Baldwin Kashe, Homer Yanozha, Milton Yanozha, unidentified boy.* Seated in front: *Lula Kaydizinne. Courtesy Frisco Native American Museum*

Apache children after four months at the Carlisle Indian School. Seated, left to right: *Ernest Hogee, Humphrey Escharzay, Beatrice Kiahtel, Janette Pahgostatum, Bishop Eatennah, Basil Ekarden.* Standing, left to right: *Samson Noran, Margaret Y. Nadasthilah, Frederick Eskelsejah, Clement Seanilzay, Hugh Chee. Photo by J. N. Choate, Carlisle, Pa., 1887. Courtesy Smithsonian Institution, National Anthropological Archives*

◀ *Apache children arriving at the Carlisle Indian School from Fort Marion, Florida, November 4, 1886.* Front row, left to right: *Clement Seanilzay, Beatrice Kiahtel, Janette Pahgostatum, Margaret Y. Nadasthilah, Frederick Eskelsejah.* Back row, left to right: *Humphrey Escharzay, Samson Noran, Hugh Chee, Basil Ekarden, Bishop Eahtennah, Ernest Hogee. Photo by J. N. Choate, Carlisle, Pa., 1886. Courtesy Smithsonian Institution, National Anthropological Archives*

Apache Squaw and papoose, 1886

Apache cradleboard, with baby, tied to Indian's back.
Courtesy Western History Collections, University of Oklahoma Library

Indian cradleboard hanging from tree; possibly burial for baby. Courtesy Smithsonian Institution

Apache baby in carrier, 1903. Photo by Edward S. Curtis, courtesy Library of Congress

Blossom Wratten Haozous, daughter of George Wratten and Chiricahua wife Annie and future wife of Sam Haozous. Courtesy Frisco Native American Museum

Chiricahua Apache women washing clothes in a stream, Fort Sill. Courtesy Frisco Native American Museum

House at Whitetail, Mescalero Reservation, New Mexico, ca. 1915. Lone man in photo may be Rogers Toklanny. Courtesy Frisco Native American Museum

Leaving Fort Sill for Mescalero, early April, 1913. Courtesy Frisco Native American Museum

Vera Shanta modeling her puberty ceremony dress, ca. 1948. Courtesy Robert S. Ove ▶

◀ *Unidentified Chiricahua Apache bride in traditional wedding costume. Courtesy Frisco Native American Museum*

Chiricahua Apache home, ca. 1883.
Courtesy Frisco Native American Museum

Apache Indian camp, Arizona. Courtesy Smithsonian Institution

◄ *This brush dwelling is commonly called a wickiup, built by Apache women in about three days. Oak or willow poles are anchored in the ground and bound with yucca-leaf strands, then covered with bundles of grass. Note also the excellent basketry shown here. Photo by Edward S. Curtis, 1903, courtesy Library of Congress*

Apache Indian tents, wickiups, and other structures at Indian camp, Mount Vernon Barracks, Alabama, ca. 1890. Courtesy U.S. Army Military History Institute

Apache prisoners being transported to Florida. Geronimo and Naiche in front ▶
row, third and fourth from right. Lozen in top row, third from right. Naiche's wife, Ha-o-zinne, top row, center. Courtesy Smithsonian Institution

Group of captive Apaches at Fort Bowie. Woman at the far left is covering her nose which is gone, an Apache punishment for adultery. Courtesy Western History Collections, University of Oklahoma Library

Mildred Imach Cleghorn, June, 1990. Photo by author

Mildred Imach Cleghorn,
chairperson, Fort Sill Apache
Tribe, 1989 Outstanding
Indian of the Year. Photo
courtesy author

Mildred Cleghorn and bust of
Cochise, August 6, 1989. Photo
by author

Mildred Imach Cleghorn, August 6, 1989. Photo by author

Mildred (left) and Myrtle Imach. Courtesy Fort Sill Museum

Unidentified Chiricahua Apache woman.
Courtesy Frisco Native American Museum

CHAPTER 5

Yesterday's Warrior Women

While most Chiricahua Apache women obeyed traditions, four women in particular—Siki, Gouyen, Dahteste, and Lozen—from time to time broke the ancient cultural restrictions pertaining to women. These Apaches surely followed some of the rules, but they also ventured outside customary women's behavior and achieved something "exceptional."[1]

The daughter of Warm Springs Apache[2] Chief Loco, Siki Toklanni was born about 1866 and grew up like the other girls—learning mainly about the ways of women but taking part in the boys' training also. Little is known about her youth until she came into the spotlight in October, 1880, at Tres Castillos, Mexico. Dragged from her horse and tied to a tree during the massacre of Chief Victorio's band by Mexicans, Siki was one of about a hundred women and children captured and marched to Chihuahua City where she was sold into slavery.[3] Her new owner, a maguey farmer, then forced her to walk to Mexico City where she remained in servitude to him for five years. Siki's childhood training in the ways of the warriors remained in her mind and caused her always to think about an escape. She and three other captive Apache women who worked on the same maguey farm bided their time and when the opportunity was right, they fled on foot, carrying only knives and one blanket but no food and no water. By moonlight two nights later Siki spied an animal skin water jug hanging from a beam above the door of a house. As the leading warrior in the group, Siki crept between barking dogs and hobbled horses toward the residence and with one swoop of her knife freed the sac. After finding water and filling the container, the women continued northward, using the stars as aids. They ate the fruit of cacti for about a week until Siki killed a rancher's calf, skinned it to obtain the hide for foot coverings, and sliced the meat for the women to carry in their clothing. Sometime during the journey homeward, a mountain lion attacked Francesca, one of the women in the small group, tearing her scalp from her head. Remembering her warrior training, Siki replaced the scalp using buckskin thongs to bind the skin to Francesca's skull. With her knife, Siki scooped sputum from the lion's mouth and rubbed it into the wounds—a Chiricahua Apache remedy proven to promote healing. The next morning the women cut leaves from a certain cactus, burned the thorns, sliced the leaves open, and applied the fleshy side to Francesca's many severe wounds. When her condition improved sufficiently, the women hid, ran, foraged, killed livestock for food, and traveled at night. A little more than three months later they were in the familiar Florida Mountains near their Arizona and New Mexico homelands where Siki located caves containing supplies that Chief Victorio had cached six years earlier. The stashed bolts of cloth and slabs of cowhide had been badly damaged by mice, but Siki salvaged what she could, sewed garments with plant fibers and animal sinew, and crafted moccasins using a sharpened bone awl. At last the women made their way to a friendly trader at Monticello, New Mexico, learned the whereabouts of their people, and then returned to the band. It had been a journey of more than a thousand miles on foot.[4]

Soon after being reunited with her people, Siki married scout Rogers Toklanni. Both of them were incarcerated by the United States government in 1886 and, upon release from confinement, they lived at Whitetail on the Mescalero Apache Reservation. Local resident Ken Bonnell remembered Siki as a short, slightly stocky woman with a wrinkled brown face and long gray hair. He recalled that she always wore long dresses, carried an old flour sack instead of a purse, and walked with the aid of a walking stick made from the limb of a tree. Bonnell characterized Siki as a warm and friendly person with a quick smile and a kind word, and he recalled a personal encounter with her that happened when, at the age of twelve, he started to work in his grandfather's general store in the nearby town of Tularosa. Bonnell wrote, "I was assigned to the front corner of the store behind the candy counter and soda pop cooler. I sold candy, soda pop, shoe polish, and all the tobacco products. The bins in the bottom of the glass fronted candy counter were always stocked with the hard candies most kids associated with Christmas. Chocolate bars and chewing gum were scarce because of the war and strictly rationed out when we were lucky enough to get a box of Hershey bars or Milky Ways. Most of our Indian customers preferred the hard candy and usually bought some when they came down from the reservation at Mescalero. As I recall, a quarter would buy about half a pound.

"It was the second Saturday of September and my second Saturday on my new job when Mrs. Toklanni came waddling through the front door of the store, her walking stick clanking out the cadence of her short, rapid steps. She approached the candy counter smiling in anticipation. 'May I help you, ma'am?' I asked, having been trained to be very courteous to our customers. When she didn't reply I automatically switched to Spanish and repeated my inquiry. She looked up and replied 'Dulce [candy].' I asked which one she wanted. She tapped the counter in front of the ribbon candy and replied 'Este [this].' When I asked how much she wanted she replied 'Naakijali [Apache for a quarter's worth].' I carefully set the scale for a half of a pound and placed a scoop full of candy in the hopper. When the scale didn't move, I dumped in another scoopful, causing the scale to pass the balance point with a thud. When I started to remove the excess candy from the hopper the old lady let out a scream that made my hair stand on end. She continued screaming at me in Apache while waving her walking stick like a war club. Startled and terrified, I just stood there wide eyed and mouth agape, fearing for my life. One of the older clerks heard the commotion and came running. On learning what had transpired, he grabbed a handful of candy and threw it into the hopper causing it again to thud past the balance point. Mrs. Toklanni's face broke into a broad smile and she lowered her walking stick, signifying her satisfaction with the amended transaction. When Mrs. Toklanni left the store, the clerk explained that when something went into the scale's hopper, be it candy, beans, or spuds, the excess was never removed when waiting on one of the older Indian ladies.

"A month passed before I waited on this venerable old lady again and I was most careful to bring the scale to an exact balance. Then with a flourish I flipped in a couple more pieces, making the scale thud past the balance, and bringing on a big smile of appreciation."[5]

Elbys Hugar, the great-granddaughter of Cochise and a Mescalero Apache Reservation resident, also remembered this woman warrior. Said

Elbys, "I used to see Siki and her husband Toklanni when I went with my parents down the road. On the side of the hill they played cards, *kunkan* mostly, out in the open. It's a very enjoyable game. We go to Juarez, Mexico, and buy the cards. Siki and her husband had a daughter, Emma, that I remember. Siki was a very nice lady. She spoke the Chiricahua language in a tone of voice that made you want to hear more and more."[6]

Siki Toklanni's Aunt Gouyen—her name means wise woman—was born about 1857. Twenty-two years later in a raid on her Apache camp in 1879 Comanches killed Gouyen's first husband. Seeking revenge, a furious and heartsick young woman left the campsite wearing her puberty ceremony buckskin dress and carrying only a water jug and dried meat. Calling upon the warrior training she received as a young girl, she followed the enemy trail on foot for four nights before she found the Comanche camp. Hiding in the dark in a safe position, she spied her husband's scalp in the chief's possession. She slipped into a circle of frenzied dancers celebrating the raid, flirted with the chief by firelight and lured him away into the shadows. After a brief and bloody struggle, Gouyen disemboweled him with his own knife. Then, holding the weapon steady, she avenged her husband's death even more by scalping the chief. Taking his breechclout and his moccasins, she galloped a stolen horse for two days back to her camp, where she collapsed into the arms of her dead husband's parents, her puberty dress stained and smeared with the Comanche chief's dried blood. When she revived, she presented her in-laws with the trophies—the Comanche's scalp, his clothing, and his footwear.[7]

A few years later Gouyen survived the massacre at Tres Castillos and avoided capture by the Mexican soldiers. Running and hiding, she and her son Kaywaykla[8] [named by Chief Victorio] barely escaped, but the fate of her infant daughter was never learned. As a young widow, she subsequently married the Apache warrior Kaytennae and in at least one instance her fighting skills saved his life. On the move from an enemy, Kaytennae dropped into an arroyo, followed by Gouyen and Kaywaykla. Moments later Gouyen saw the shadow of another weapon's barrel point toward her husband. Reacting instantly, she shot at and killed the man who was ready to kill Kaytennae. In 1886 this family too was imprisoned with the other Chiricahuas. Gouyen died in 1903 and is buried in the Apache prisoner-of-war cemetery at Fort Sill, Oklahoma, amid members of the Kaywaykla family.

A third woman warrior, Dahteste, was small in stature but large in experience. Born about 1860, she was a sister of Chiricahua sub-chief Chihuahua's wife Ilth-goz-ay. As a child Dahteste and her family rode with Cochise, a memory she carried throughout her life. She married Ahnandia, one of Geronimo's warriors, and fought beside him in the many battles with the military. Geronimo called upon Dahteste and her best friend Lozen to become messengers, an important job in the group. Only trusted individuals became messengers, for if information was not delivered or passed on accurately, many lives could be lost—Apache lives. Together with Lozen, Dahteste was responsible for initiating the negotiations with the U.S. Army that led to Geronimo's surrender in 1886. She and Ahnandia were imprisoned with the other Chiricahuas, and sometime during the confinement she "divorced" Ahnandia in the "Indian way." Records do not reveal who left whom, or the reasons, but it did not take too long for her to find her next husband, the widower scout named Coonie [also spelled Kuni]. Dahteste and Coonie survived incarceration and were released in 1913 to make their home at Whitetail on the Mescalero Apache Reservation. Having no children of their own, they raised Coonie's three from a previous marriage to a woman named Betier [who died at Fort Sill], one of his nephews, and two other orphaned children.

Dahteste never lost the fiery spirit that had characterized her life, as author Eve Ball discovered on a bitterly cold day in January, 1949. Dahteste and her niece Eliza Coonie[9] had driven in Eliza's wide-open pickup truck from their home at Whitetail to Ruidoso, where Ball lived. Sometime during the day Dahteste had become ill and Eliza stopped at Ball's home for help. Both women were half frozen, for an unexpected snowstorm had come up, and they were not dressed warmly. After they thawed out and drank some hot tea, Mrs. Ball invited them to spend the night. They refused but agreed to take her heavy blankets and gloves with them, as well as an old seal cape that had belonged to Mrs. Ball's late mother. When Eliza and Dahteste realized the wrap had come from a dead person, Dahteste demanded that Eliza take it off her. They threw it in the snow at Mrs. Ball's feet and drove away.[10] That was Mrs. Ball's first experience with the Chiricahua taboo against the use of anything that had belonged to the dead and with the volatility of a woman warrior.

Elbys Hugar also remembered Dahteste when she was a very old woman. "I used to see her around the reservation," Elbys said. "Dahteste was always dressed nicely in her Apache clothing. She wore beautiful beads, turquoise sometimes, and a very pretty belt. I always admired her beaded bags. She wore her hair straight. Just brushed it out. I don't think I ever saw her braid her hair. She was a nice looking woman, very nice looking."[11]

Before Dahteste died of old age, Robert S. Ove, who in 1948 was a young teacher at Whitetail, taught Dauphin Coonie, Dahteste's great-granddaughter. "Can you tell me something about her?" Ove asked the girl, adding, "She must be very old." Dauphin responded with a blank stare that Ove thought was out of awe and respect for her relatives and astonishment at his nerve to ask the question. Ove also recalled, "The closest I got to her [Dahteste] was one day when an attorney from the Bureau of Indian Affairs came to [the reservation] to determine whether the tribe had grounds for filing any claims for the land that had been taken from them. One of the witnesses was Old Lady Coonie [a term of respect used by most when referring to Dahteste]. She refused to speak English. In her guttural, clipped Athapascan dialect the wizened old woman told of the early days when there were no 'white-eyes' in most of Arizona and New Mexico. Her stony-faced niece [Eliza] acted as her interpreter. She mumbled the answers in response to the questions, deliberately making the bureaucratic questioner quite uneasy and enjoying every moment of it. For all her age, the old lady was full of wit. I stopped by the chapel once when the women were meeting and I could hear her mumble something about me. Everyone else burst out laughing."[12]

Of these women warriors, Dahteste's friend Lozen is perhaps the most familiar and the woman herself surely the most intriguing. For years researchers have been unsuccessfully trying to learn more about her, but she still remains mysterious, especially because the Chiricahuas to this day protect her and the oral history about her that has been privately passed on within Apache families through the generations. After nearly twenty years of hearing bits and pieces about her, it was just during the 1998 puberty ceremonial that I learned an intimate detail of her life: Chief Victorio's pet name for her. He called her "little sister," which in the Apache language sounds like "she-la-ziyah." Yes, indeed she was that, but she was also much, much more.

Born sometime in the late 1840s[13] into the Warm Springs Chiricahua band, Lozen was raised as other girls. I would not be surprised if she balked at the women's mundane duties, but she would not have been allowed to complain too much before her mother stopped her. More than likely Lozen also underwent some of the training offered to boys as well. Preferring to imitate Victorio,[14] as a young girl she leaped from boulders, sliced the air with her knife, yelled, rode bareback on a stallion and wore a bandanna to hold back her long black hair. When Victorio became a noted chief, Lozen was one of his most trusted warriors and a full participant in warring and raiding.

Lozen was an excellent horsewoman and quite skilled at stealing horses, traits necessary for the Chiricahuas to remain a free people. Frequently fulfilling the duties of both an Apache woman and a warrior, she was especially close to the other women and children in Victorio's band and often took responsibility for their well-being. In the 1880 breakout from the San Carlos Reservation, for example, Lozen led the women and children across a river to safety from the U.S. Army's pursuit, and then returned to help the men fight the soldiers. A few years later, on the Warm Springs Reservation in New Mexico, she rode through steep canyon walls and across a meandering stream at the head of a party of frightened women and children on horses, guiding them off the reservation to temporary freedom from the enforced military administration of their homelands. I have walked and driven a pickup truck through this narrow passageway and stopped to imagine the sounds and confusion that occurred there more than one hundred years ago. The stream is still running between the canyon walls and watercress grows freely in the cold water. A Chiricahua Apache medicine woman I was with gathered one or two special stones from the stream bed for use back at Mescalero during her healing ceremonies. I knew enough not to question her about the stones, so when she caught me rudely staring at her, I simply acknowledged her activities with a nod of my head and, embarrassed, looked away. I could not help but wonder if those particular stones watched Lozen lead the Apache women and children to safety a century and more ago.

During the years 1860–80, the government was conducting extensive roundups of all Indian peoples across the country. For natives who dared resist the plan, death or incarceration seemed to be the only alternatives. First though, the Native Americans had to be subdued, an action that the Warm Springs Chiricahua Apaches successfully resisted for many years due, in part, to Lozen's skill in warfare. Fearless at times, she dashed on horseback through hails of Army bullets to fulfill strategic goals, knew the correct herbs to apply to warriors' wounds to effect quick healing, assisted young women giving birth in the middle of battles or during more peaceful times, and, without hesitating, took part in the slaughter of more than two hundred Mexicans in revenge for Victorio's death. Informed speculation argues that had Lozen been near Victorio at the time of the October, 1880, massacre by Mexican soldiers at Tres Castillos, Mexico, and exercised her unusual gift from *Ussen,* he and more than a hundred members of his band might not have perished.

Through supernatural ability believed to have begun during her puberty ceremony, Lozen could tell the direction from which the enemy was coming. Climbing to the top of a mesa or a similar high point, Lozen would lift her hands and arms high and pray:

> *Upon the earth*
> *On which we live*
> *Ussen has Power.*
> *This Power he grants me*
> *For locating the enemy.*
> *I search for that enemy*
> *Which only Ussen, Creator of Life*
> *Can reveal to me.*

Lozen then moved slowly in a clockwise direction, stopping only when a tingling feeling or change in the color of her palms was noticeable. The direction she faced when she stopped was usually where the enemy was located. Occasionally the sensation became so intense that her palms turned purple, meaning that the enemy was very near. The farther away the foe, the weaker her reaction.

In those days, if you were an American or Mexican soldier chasing the Apaches and your luck had run out, Lozen would more than likely use this Power to find you. You could not mistake her; she would be the only woman riding toward you among the leaders. If you were able to safely step aside and watch, she would impress you with her horsemanship and grace. But you could not expect any mercy from this particular Apache. That was not her style. Under expert leadership, the Chiricahuas did their best to control the numbers of people chasing them. One favorite technique, often used by Lozen, was to shoot the horses out from under their Mexican or American riders. Then, obviously, it did not take long to put an end to the terror felt by the soldiers or civilians frantically scurrying on foot for their lives. Lozen was a very willing participant in these activities, riding confidently into any battle and, on the killing ground, insuring that she got her fair share of the action.

However, years before the earth became soaked with the blood of red men and white men, Victorio consulted with Lozen, obtained her concurrence, and then tried to negotiate a separate peace on behalf of his Warm Springs band. His people wanted to live in southwestern New Mexico, on a reservation of their own, surrounded by the familiar hills and valleys they loved best of all. That was their homeland, Victorio told the Americans, and if the government would assign the Warm Springs people to that area, he promised they would cause no more trouble. It was not to be. Instead, in 1877 Victorio and his people were moved to the San Carlos Apache Reservation in Arizona where they were forced to live among strangers, some of whom were their adversaries. They endured as long as they could and then more than three hundred frustrated Warm Springs Apaches took matters into their own hands and literally stampeded their way out of San Carlos. After stealing some Army horses, they headed east, led by Victorio and Lozen, free to be themselves for a while before the government rounded them up again. Until then, however, they could live as they pleased and ride with the wind across the countryside they loved so dearly.

With a little imagination, you can see it now. Rifle held high over her head, Lozen kicks her horse in his ribs after they both had rested a moment, out of breath beside a busy stream. When the horse reaches the far bank, Lozen calls to the others, those women and children still hesitating on the other side. Her encouraging words overcome their fright and, one by one or sometimes with the children riding double, the women cautiously force their horses into the rushing water. A few minutes later, safely beside Lozen, the youngsters calm down and the women feel the security of the solid earth once more beneath their horses' feet. Lozen then speaks to the group in a firm voice. She is on her way, she says, to join the rest of the warriors, now confident that the women and children with her will have no trouble getting back to their camp. The enemy is gone, she tells them, and the warriors are in the hills, protecting the people from afar. Lozen softly nods before leaving. With a wave of her hand, she rides off, eager to help the men guard the small band.

Because Lozen was unmarried, she was able to ride with the men and simultaneously take care of the women and children. During one memorable battle, she crawled through the line of intense fire to rescue an ammunition pouch containing more than five hundred cartridges that had been dropped by another warrior. Lozen retrieved the pouch and returned to the battle unscathed.

Through all her exploits, however, she may have carried a vision in her heart of a special warrior, one whom no mortal could rival or equal. Soon after her puberty ceremony, many young men wanted to marry her, but she refused. Victorio, as head of the family, did not force her to do otherwise. After that, Apache folklore relates that Lozen saw someone who came to be called the "Gray Ghost." Legend tells of this warrior, handsome and powerful, riding alone on a magnificent stallion in the arroyos and on the mesas throughout Apacheria. The Gray Ghost, during one of his rides, actually came into the Warm Springs camp and spent time with the people. He told Victorio that he too was a chief but from another land, far away toward the east. Then a wagon passed nearby as they were conversing. Twelve men who were neither Indian nor Mexican nor American guarded it. Inside the wagon sat a beautiful young woman attended by an old wrinkled hag who might even have been a witch. As the wagon continued westward, the handsome chief rode his steed after it and was never seen again by the Warm Springs Apache people. However, it is said that Lozen remembered him fondly and despite her close associations with many brave warriors, she never found one appealing enough to overcome her longing for the Gray Ghost of her youth.[15]

It is possible that from time to time Lozen became tired of fulfilling dual roles or living two lives, one as a warrior and one as a Chiricahua woman [although she probably did not fulfill too many of the usual women's tasks]. But, being Apache, she gave no sign of discontent. As a warrior, Lozen would have gladly followed any instructions given her by the chief. Without question, if he wanted her to fight, she could be the ruthless equal of any man. If it were his wish that she stay away from the action and help the more dependent members of the small band, she willingly did so. Nonetheless, if she had her way, Lozen definitely preferred being with the warriors in the thick of a good battle. With Lozen present, the Warm Springs band knew they need not fear a surprise attack whether they were camped, on a raid, or riding as a war party. If there were even a hint of danger, Lozen would find it when asked by the chief to "make medicine" and sing her song to *Ussen*.

At the end of her freedom there was no need for Lozen to use her superior fighting skills or her power. At some point after Victorio's death she had joined Geronimo's band and he, in 1886, was well aware of the limited alternatives offered the Apache people who were still free.[16] Some of Geronimo's warriors at first refused to listen to his logic about the possibility of surrender. Others, those weary of constantly fighting to stay alive were eager to be with their women and children already imprisoned in Florida. After carefully considering the circumstances and the warriors' various points of view, Geronimo sent Lozen and Dahteste to arrange a meeting with the Americans.[17] Long negotiations, promises, and compromises led to a bloodless surrender [that was not to happen for another six months], a decision Geronimo later said he would regret for the rest of his life.

Lozen was imprisoned with the Chiricahuas, first in Florida and then in Alabama. Almost nothing is known of her activities while incarcerated except that she caught the "coughing sickness," tuberculosis, and died on June 17, 1889. According to the U.S. Army, she is buried in an unmarked grave at the prison site in Mount Vernon, Alabama.[18] In death Lozen's spirit became free to roam over the land she loved so much and fought so hard to protect. It must have been a welcome change from confinement.

CHAPTER 6

Today's Warrior Woman

Mildred Imach Cleghorn

Do exceptional Apache women still exist as we approach the twenty-first century? After all, these days they need not escape from slavery and find their way more than one thousand miles back to their campsite, as Siki did. They need not avenge a killing as brutally as Gouyen did. They need not become messengers from the tribe to the U.S. Army, as Dahteste did. And they need not pray from a high place to protect their people, as Lozen did. Still, one special attribute has remained: the enduring Chiricahua Apache spirit.

No longer expressed in warfare, the spirit now shows itself in leadership. Descendants of yesterday's leaders of both genders are today's community health representatives, medicine men and medicine women, managers of major tribal projects, directors of cultural centers and libraries, and members in high positions on church boards. Many oversee programs such as those that distribute commodities or are involved in running senior centers. Some are educators holding administrative positions, or teaching the Apache language and other classes in reservation schools. Others work with legislative committees on the federal and state government levels. A designated few periodically address members of Congress in Washington on behalf of their people. One or two meet with presidents. Importantly, the grandchildren and great-grandchildren of the celebrated chiefs and warriors of old are the elected chairmen and chairwomen of the contemporary Chiricahua Apaches. Mildred Imach Cleghorn, former chairperson of the Fort Sill Chiricahua/

Warm Springs Apache Tribe for twenty years, stood out as an example of modern leadership in which the indomitable Apache spirit remained alive and well.

Mildred's heritage can be traced back only as far as her paternal grandmother, the woman called Go-lah-at-tsa, who was born in 1854 into the Warm Springs Apache group during a time when men like Mangas Coloradas and Cochise were in their prime. Her playmates could have been Gouyen and Lozen; she might have known about little Siki's birth. When the Warm Springs folks got together with Cochise's band to celebrate puberty ceremonies or on other special occasions, it is possible that young Dahteste joined the girls.

More than likely Go-lah-at-tsa had a different name in her youth, for her name means "did many things," which sounds like a designation that would come later in life. About 1879 she became the first wife of Clee-neh and the mother of Richard [whose Apache name was En-ohn], born in 1883, and Gertrude, born one year later. Both these children were eventually sent to the Carlisle School in Pennsylvania, where Richard participated in the outing program. A story tells that he spent summers on a local farm run by a family named Imach and liked them so much [the feeling was mutual] that he took their last name as his own. Richard stayed for three years at Carlisle, from about 1897–1900, and then took a train back to the prisoner-of-war camp at Fort Sill. It was there that he met and married Amy Wratten, who was born at the Alabama incarceration site in 1890 and was transferred in 1894 with the other prisoners of war to Oklahoma. [Amy was one of the two daughters of George Wratten,[1] the white interpreter-supervisor of the Apache prisoners, and his first wife, Annie. Although daughters of a non-Indian, the Wratten girls, Amy and Blossom, considered themselves to be Chiricahua Apache prisoners of war and remained confined in the camps where they grew up and attended school with their relatives and friends.]

Two daughters, Mildred and Myrtle, were born into the Imach marriage; Myrtle died in infancy. Having been educated "in the white man's way," Mildred's parents were naturals to remain in Oklahoma upon release from incarceration in 1914.[2] With their three-year-old daughter they became farmers and citizens in good standing of Apache, Oklahoma,[3] but surely had not forgotten the stories they had heard about their outstanding heritage as Warm Springs Chiricahua Apaches.

Their Indian group called themselves the "*Chihennes*," or Red Paint People and lived in the mountain ranges west of New Mexico's Rio

Grande. The Warm Springs band of Chiricahuas and its activities came to an abrupt end in October, 1880, when most of them and their chief, Victorio, were killed by Mexicans in an ambush at Tres Castillos, a mountain range in northern Mexico. Mildred's surviving ancestors then melded into one of the other groups of Chiricahuas, although any information about the linear descent of this family until the middle 1800s has been lost to history. With the surrender of Geronimo in 1886, the surviving Warm Springs people became prisoners of war, as did all the Chiricahuas.

"With one or two exceptions, I don't remember what it was like for us when we lived [as prisoners of war] at Fort Sill," Mildred said. Even a return trip to the site would not stimulate recollections, she believed, because the broad field where her family's house stood in a small prisoner village now looks so much different than it once did. Overgrown, abandoned, lonely, one would never know the place was once home to nearly a dozen Apache families. The current occupants—wild knee-high grasses, delicate pale pink primrose, and pink and white verbena ground cover—moved in over time and changed the character of the terrain even more. The view in every direction from this former prison camp site is unobstructed. Not too far away, and somewhat below the elevated tract, a stand of thick-leafed trees separates the field from a more fertile area and is about a quarter of a mile from the nearest water well. This choice location was assigned to the scout Noche's group of Apaches when they arrived at Fort Sill from Alabama in October, 1894.

Living quarters were modest. In a 1976 interview, Mildred's Aunt Blossom recalled, "The government just gave us little two room houses with a breezeway in the middle . . . looked something like a narrow carport. We'd cook in one side and sleep in the other. If it was a big family, you used both rooms to eat, cook, and sleep in." Because there were no storage facilities for food or anything else, the families ". . . put nails in the walls and hung those bags [containing dried food such as corn] on the walls. You just put them in bags and hung 'em around in the house. Everything you wanted to get out of your way, you hung on the walls."[4]

As youngsters, Amy and Blossom Wratten played with other Chiricahua children, and the girls dearly loved their dolls. "We used to make plain old rag dolls," said Blossom. "We didn't know much about the kind of dolls they have now; we just made dolls and played like they were our babies."[5] Amy Imach's love for dolls continued long into her adult years, including when she became a mother herself. Mildred remembered, "My Mama made little rag dolls the same way Apache women have always done and we would have whole families of these dolls. She would take a square of cloth, roll it up, and then fold it in half. Then she'd take another square, roll it up and make it look like arms and legs. Then she tied them so the doll had arms, legs, and a head. They were Indian dolls. Then we sewed clothes for them—just little skirts and blouses. Mama showed me how and that's how I started."[6]

I have seen and held in my hands a doll that Amy made just about one hundred years ago. She dressed the doll in a Chiricahua Apache ceremonial buckskin dress, an exact replica of those worn by Apache maidens during their puberty ceremony. Superbly crafted, it shows only slight evidence of aging. The doll's dress is fringed with dozens of slices of tanned hide. Red beads outline the hem of the dress just before the fringe emerges. She wears traditional Chiricahua Apache moccasins, thigh-high, and folded downward over and over to serve as carry-alls. The tips just beyond the toes are turned upward, an Apache characteristic specifically tailored to protect wearers.

The doll carries a hide pouch as her purse, decorated with a round shield created from red, white, and blue beads, with beaded fringes of the same color. Apache maidens today carry sacred pollen in pouches like these during the enactment of ancient puberty rituals. Around her neck is row after row of a necklace of tiny black and white beads, a favorite of many Chiricahua Apache women. Earrings made from red and white beads hang from the places her ears would be, and a feather has been sewn into a traditional maiden's headpiece crafted from leather and blue and red beads. A red cloth cape drapes from the back of the dress in customary Chiricahua fashion. Mildred often displayed this antique Apache doll as the centerpiece of her collection along with the many Chiricahua Apache dolls she continued to craft.

Amy's doll traveled with the young family in 1914 from Fort Sill to their first home in Apache. "My memory really begins on the farm," Mildred said. "We drove in a hack and as we came over the hill, there was a slope downward. I will never forget coming up over that hill on the south side, where the road now is, and my father telling us that was where we were going to live. Down in the valley. There was a three room house and a barn and a lot. I remember my father saying, 'This will be our home. This is where we're going to live from now on.' That's where we started."[7] The spot was just outside of Apache, Oklahoma.

That small farm town officially came into being through a land lottery held in Lawton, Oklahoma, on October 12, 1901. Prior to that time there were no buildings, just rickety shacks here and there. Apache actually began at Richards Spur, ten miles south of the present town, and before long the first commercial building, a bank, was started. The population increased slowly and spread northward. In 1913, when release from confinement was imminent, the prisoners of war who had opted to remain in Oklahoma were permitted to look for land under trust in the vicinity of Fort Sill. These homesites could be purchased from the families of deceased Comanches, Kiowas, and Kiowa-Apaches. "When we knew the plots were for sale, my Daddy and others went looking around to see which place they wanted to buy. That's the way it was done," said Mildred in May of 1992. Each selected parcel had to be approved by the Bureau of Indian Affairs and was bought using moneys held in what was called the "Apache Trust Fund." Comprising this escrow account were the funds from the sale of the Apache cattle the men had tended and run at Fort Sill. Because the Apaches were excellent cattlemen, the beef was high quality and brought a good price on the market. "Each adult was given $3000 and each child was given $2000 from the fund," Mildred said. "We were supposed to buy land with the money, . . . but the allotments were not allowed to be contiguous. The Benedict Johze family [a leader of the group] lived twelve miles out. My relatives, the Haozous family, were six miles away. It was hard for us to get from one place to another . . . Our people chose allotments that had creeks or streams running through. The supervisor tried to tell them they should choose parcels that were solid land, but our people wanted water somewhere on the land."

Life in freedom began for three-year-old Mildred Imach with a contagious disease. "The next thing I remember [after reaching the family's new home] was when I had the measles soon after we came there. We were expecting a new colt and I never will forget when my Daddy came and told me we had a new horse. I wanted to see it so badly, but in those days when we had measles we had to put the shades down and protect our eyes in a darkened room. So there I was, sitting inside with the sun shining outside. Mama and my daddy didn't want me to see the colt because they were afraid the light would affect my eyes. In the evening when the sun went down they brought the colt around so I could look out the window and see it. He was a workhorse and was my Father's pride and joy."[8]

Like many other farm girls, young Mildred's chores included chasing after the family's cows and milking them, keeping the chickens happy, gardening, and harvesting cotton. She hated picking cotton so much that she vowed she would make something of herself. Apparently her parents had the same idea. "My mother and father and older folks used to say, 'Well, look around you. There's not an Indian who lives nearby. You have nothing but white people here. You have to go to school.' That's all I ever heard. 'You've got to learn the white man's way and you've got to do it a little bit more if you can, because you have to fight all the time for whatever you get, for whatever you want. . . . Education, education, education.'" In their eyes, education in "the white man's way" and the subsequent use of that knowledge was the key to success. So, the Apache spirit took a turn in the Imach family toward their captors' way of life and values.

Taking her family's advice to heart, the little girl faithfully rode a horse to school every day and remembers being a first grader in the Apache public school system. World War I was tearing up Europe then, and Mildred helped the war effort in elementary school by making bandages from sheets and by finding and saving cold cream jars for medicine containers. At that time, quite a few Indian children were sent away from home to boarding schools, but Amy Imach, herself a product of that philosophy of education, wanted something more for her daughter. Mildred recalled her mother's strong words. "She said, 'I don't want any child of mine going to a boarding school.' But, having grown up in public schools, I didn't know any Indian children. When I went to Indian gatherings, I was always alone. I didn't like that; I was young and I wanted to know someone."

After graduating in 1930 from public high school in Apache, Mildred decided she wanted to attend Haskell Junior College in Lawrence, Kansas, where many Native American students of her age were receiving a higher education. Her mother, however, was still against sending Mildred away. "I just begged her to go to Haskell," Mildred said, "and she finally agreed. But she said to me, 'Now the minute you get lonesome you come right home. You let me know and you can come right home.' I promised her I'd do that, but I didn't. I got so lonesome I thought I'd die, but I wouldn't tell her that. I stayed, and by the end of October, why, you couldn't drive me away."

Mildred spent two years at Haskell taking business courses, because the school no longer offered her first choice—teachers' training. Leaving Haskell in 1932, she was employed by the Bureau of Indian Affairs office in Stewart, Nevada. She worked at the job until 1937, when she became "so fed up with four walls that I just quit. My mother thought I was crazy to give up a $1440 a year job and the security, which was what she wanted for me. But that wasn't what I wanted. I like people, and I wanted to work with people. I had come to know a Bureau of Indian Affairs extension agent, a lady who visited our home all the time and I admired her. Also, my mother used to go to club meetings the extension folks sponsored, and I went with her. They always had something for us kids to do, and I really enjoyed it. I decided right there that when I got big, I wanted to do that. Extension agent work would give me a chance to meet people and I knew our Indian people needed that type of help too—home living, home situations like childcare, cooking, sewing, and home economics in general. I saw how my people lived and I wanted to help them."[9]

Because she did not have the necessary academic background required to be an extension agent, Mildred went back to school in 1937 to study home economics at Oklahoma A&M University [now called Oklahoma State University]. True to form, her favorite courses were those concerned with family life and child development. Immediately after she earned a bachelor of science degree and graduated in August, 1941, her professional life began. She taught school for a year and a half, but to get into the occupation she wanted, Mildred "had to teach home economics for two years. They let me go sooner because there was a job opening in Kansas. They asked me if I would take it and I said, 'Sure.'

"I worked on a Kansas reservation with the Potawatomi, Kickapoo, Iowa, and Sac and Fox people. . . . The whole reservation was my working territory. I was involved in 4-H Club work with children in the day schools, and in organizing clubs at each one of them. The Kickapoos had a 4-H Club that had a children's program in which they chose what they wanted to do—a calf project, or gardening—whatever they wanted. Usually they ended up with an exhibit that showed what they accomplished. I thought that was good for our Indian children. It taught them how to conduct a club meeting with parliamentary procedure, and how to have a timely topic prepared when they gave speeches."[10]

As an extension agent, Mildred lived off the reservation in nearby Horton for the entire period she worked in Kansas—four years—and, always a religious woman, she joined the Methodist Church. Not too much later she was invited by the church's women's guild to speak to them and describe her work. It was a welcome invitation, for, as she had gotten to know the church women, [all of whom were white], she realized that they had absolutely no idea about the differences among Native Americans. "I was just floored," said Mildred. "They thought we could all understand one another, and that when you spoke Indian, you spoke in a common language, and everybody understood. But it's not that way at all. So, I thought, 'Well, since I'm working with women as an extension agent on the reservation, and have this opportunity to go out and talk [to Methodist women] about Indians, I wonder how I can show them that we Indian people are so different from one another, how we have our own language and our own philosophies of life.' The next thing I came up with was to demonstrate our differences through showing our clothes, and the way Indian women dress. Most of the men, except for Plains Indians, dress similarly, but women don't. I decided to make dolls so people could see that we women are not alike—none of us. I made a Kickapoo doll first and then four more. Later I decided to make one doll for each of the tribes that I would work with in my career. And that's how I got started on my lifelong ambition and avocation. I haven't accomplished my goal yet. I've made 40 dolls out of a total of 72 that I want to make. These days there's very little memory of the original dresses and other clothing. Modern Indian women wear necklaces from one tribe, belts from another, moccasins from a third, and so on. Also, many young women today have left their culture and become part of the mainstream, so traditional wear is in danger of becoming part of the past. I like to preserve the richness of all Indian cultures by dressing my dolls in the old-fashioned way."[11]

Along with her job and her hobby, as a young, attractive woman, Mildred had many suitors, but one man in particular held her interest. He was Bill Cleghorn, a Pawnee, whom she met while working in the Pawnee area in Kansas. Mildred and Bill were married in the Dutch Reformed Church on the Mescalero Apache Reservation, and, because they never had any children of their own, they adopted Penny, a young girl from Mescalero. After Bill's untimely death, Mildred never remarried. Her full-time job and dollmaking kept her "too busy," she said. All through the years she worked as an extension agent—four years in Pawnee, Oklahoma, two years in Clinton, Oklahoma, and two years on the Mescalero Apache Reservation in New Mexico—she continued crafting dolls. She would come home from work very tired, but as soon as she sat down at the sewing machine, her vitality returned.

The sewing room before she died resembled those of her past—a pot-pourri of paraphernalia gathered through Mildred's lifetime hobby of creating dolls. Ermine tails, buttons of all sizes, cowrie shells, multicolored cloths and threads, boxes full of treasured items, rolls of baby rickrack, pieces of tanned hides, bright beads, books about craftwork and American Indian tribal histories, a small sewing machine that seemed nearly invisible because it was overwhelmed by the number of supplies, a file cabinet, an old comfortable single bed with a sagging mattress and whatever else she needed to fulfill her creative urges were kept here.

After a long career serving Indian people from many tribes, she returned to her "roots" in 1965 when she retired from an active professional life and moved onto her property. Looking down a dirt road from the driveway, she saw the original three-room structure she and her family had shared in 1914 after release from incarceration.[12] Taking a few days' rest, the next thing Mildred did after she retired was to go to the countryside around Apache and dig up a sapling to plant near the driveway of her brick house. She was not sure if the transplant would live or die, but she wanted somehow to commemorate the beginning of the next phase of her life. The healthy tree now spreads its branches and offers shade to automobiles, people, and dogs—not necessarily in that order and not necessarily all at once. Dogs have always been essential to traditional Apaches. In days long gone, they served as pack animals and, when not following the seasons or the hunt with the tribe, they were also four-legged companions to children and adults alike. Within Chiricahua circles, a story tells about the people being so fond of their dogs that when the prisoners left Fort Sill for the last time on their way to the Mescalero Apache Reservation, women hid their dogs under their skirts to take them along. There was no other way to thwart the Army's prohibition against removing the animals from the military reserve. When the women were ready to detrain at Tularosa, New Mexico—a small town on the edge of the reservation—a dozen or more dogs leaped out first.

Those Apaches who remained in Oklahoma felt the same about the animals, and the fondness continues still. Mildred's dogs numbered from two to five and more at any time, depending on the fertility of the females. They were quite independent and had the run of the property, including a creek. When it got too hot in Apache, the dogs loved to take a dip and cool off. However, wet or dry, under no circumstances were they allowed in the house; that would cause way too many problems, especially in her favorite place—the sewing room—for she needed space to concentrate on her work in a noiseless setting.

Creating the dolls was never simple, especially for a talented doll-maker who demanded that the dolls wear clothing that authentically replicated a tribe's traditional dress. "I found during my research in the early years that sometimes 'authorities' were even confused as to the correctness in detail. That's when I decided that the best source of information would be knowledgeable women from each tribe. Although I hadn't planned it that way, I began making and dressing the dolls to represent my new friends I had found in the various tribes. Each doll symbolizes the woman or student from whom I obtained the information about her tribe's Indian dress," Mildred recalled in a newspaper interview.[13] Other information about traditional Indian women's clothing was available in printed material, but "Books and pictures don't always tell the whole story," she said. "A Wichita woman saw my Wichita doll some time ago and told me it wasn't right. I had braided the doll's hair, which was according to a picture I had found. The woman told me that they didn't braid their hair. When I investigated it further, I came across another photo, this one taken by Edward Curtis in 1870 that showed the Wichita women wearing no tops and using blankets for skirts. So, I had to change the body pattern, too, because my doll needed a bosom.[14] Well, there would be no way to reproduce a topless model with just flats, so I adjusted my pattern and gave my doll a bosom! I stuffed it accordingly. I think it would be nice to use it for all the rest of them because it gives them a little contour. A little more fullness."[15] And then Mildred Cleghorn threw her head back and roared.

A few minutes later she said, "For a while it wasn't popular to be an Indian, and many people weren't interested in helping me find information about various tribal clothing," she said. "I think a whole generation lost interest in their own people because they didn't want to be Indians. But I kept looking for information about the costumes Indian women wore before much contact with the white man. I went to the oldest person on each reservation where I worked and took notes of what they told me and made sketches. Then I looked in history books, but there are very few pictures of Indian women. If I did find a photo, it was just head and shoulders, so I couldn't see the skirt." A full view of the old outfits is rare also, she pointed out, because few Indian women were photographed before 1900 and then they usually stood behind their husbands. "I have taken great care to insure that the dresses are historically correct in every detail. Then I discussed my information with respected sources on historical dress, finding that where there are discrepancies it was because in later years the tribes intermingled and often modified their garb when they found another style which they thought beautiful. If I found I made a mistake, this was corrected before the doll became a permanent part of my collection."[16]

For more than half a century Mildred Cleghorn accumulated enough information and materials to create original native apparel with which to dress her dolls. Before sewing began, however, the dolls themselves had to be made. "First thing I do is make the bodies," Mildred said. "It takes me about half a day to make the body of my Apache maiden doll, just as an example. I choose a very simple pattern that I call the 'gingerbread pattern' because it's just two pieces of closely woven unbleached muslin cloth sewed together and stuffed. I used to use cotton for the stuffing, but today I prefer polyester. Cotton has little bumps and it takes more time with cotton. Then I hand tint the doll with powder paint. I rub it on with a cloth. The last thing I make is the head. Then I sew everything together, the head and all. I'm ready for the dress.

"At first I didn't put any underwear or any petticoats on my dolls. When I had about ten or twelve dolls, I was invited to a Kiwanis dinner to speak about my work and show them the dolls I'd made. The first thing the Kiwanians did was to lift the skirts and look underneath to see what the dolls were wearing. So, I decided I'd put pantaloons and a petticoat on them." She chuckled at the recollection. "If the women in the tribe the doll represents wore moccasins, I make moccasins for their feet. If they wore boots, I make boots. And I really try to use hand tanned buckskin. Too bad I can't find it around home," she said, "and I really need it because when I use a needle, it goes right through [the hand tanned buckskin] just like silk. Using the commercially tanned hides is hard work and takes the pleasure out of it. It's amazing the different ways a pair of moccasins can be cut and look alike. What intrigues me is how the first person who made moccasins came to do it. How he figured it out, how he tanned the buckskin. I have a friend in Idaho and she tells me the Indians there still do hand tanned work, so I get a few buckskins from her. After all these years she knows what I use for my dolls, and what I use for my own personal moccasins or boots. Those are made from a heavy tanned leather that is not stretched too thin."[17]

Along with difficulty in acquiring the soft leather she preferred for her dolls, Mildred had problems finding other accessories and the sewing implements necessary to complete a doll's dress. "I used size 16 beads at one time and now I can't find those long needles necessary for the beads that are so hard to work with. I have broken needles in half and sharpened points on them and used them that way, but I remember I always had trouble finding them. So I switched beads to size 13, which is a little larger. Making a bag and hair piece for my Apache maiden doll takes me about half a day, if I just sit and work without getting up and going anywhere."

The material Mildred used for a doll's black hair also changed due to outside circumstances. "My first doll, the Kickapoo, still has her yarn. I started with wool yarn and it just didn't look good at all to me and then I found purl thread, crochet thread, and I used that. It was a little finer, but I didn't like it either. So then I found darning cotton, old fashioned darning cotton. And that worked because I can just use my own hair brush and it straightens the doll's hair out. But today they've quit making that type of thread because no one darns their socks anymore, so the darning thread is altogether different from what it used to be. It's still called 'darning cotton' but it's a heavier thread so when it's braided together the strands contain more threads than before. It's stiffer, and I can't comb it with a brush. I've thought of using artificial hair, but haven't tried it yet. I want to feel it before I use it."

Cowrie shells, an important component of many Indian women's dresses, are vanishing. "I wanted one-quarter inch size," said Mildred, "so I looked through a book for a place that sells cracked shells. I wrote to every one of those stores. The only place I found was in Massachusetts, and the shop owner sent me a cupful for a dollar. Before they arrived in the mail, I was paying ten cents apiece locally, because Oklahoma is way inland [and shells of any kind are hard to get]. I almost fell over when I opened the package and saw a whole cupful for a dollar. Another thing I learned about cowrie shells is that there are variations. I think that fellow sent me six samples in three-inch bottles. The colorings and the shapes were different. He didn't know which ones to send me, so he sent them all.

"I can't get little tiny buttons anymore either. A fourth of an inch is the smallest I can find anywhere. I want authentic pearl buttons, but they're no where to be found. Maybe in an antique store. I told a woman from Dallas who represented Mattel Toys about needing those buttons and she sent me a whole bunch, but they're not pearl. They're plastic. The last time I used real pearl buttons was when I did the beadwork for the back of the Tlingit doll's blanket."

And the dress? "Sewing the dress itself takes a while. I use 36 inches of polyester blend material with a small print on it, just the little ginghams, flowers, and lines and stripes for example, for the top of the skirt and 72 inches for the bottom. Then I use a half a yard of material, 36 inches wide and I cut it in four strips for the skirt. I like baby rick-rack in three rows, so that means more than four yards on the bottom of the skirt. They have such gorgeous materials now, prints of all colors and designs."

After the clothing is complete and the doll is dressed, Mildred puts on the face. "I think I've improved on this," she said. "I don't paint them anymore. Now I embroider the face onto the tinted muslin with thread."[18] Then another doll was ready for the world. Her splendid craftwork was in demand by museums, private collectors and afficionados from coast to coast and beyond. When presenting her dolls at exhibits, Mildred took advantage of the opportunity to lecture her audiences about historical events that affected her ancestors and her tribe in modern times.

Audible gasps were often heard when Mildred, standing behind a table full of dolls in colorful native clothing, told gatherings that she was one of only a handful of surviving Chiricahua Apache prisoners of war. Her words contrasted dramatically with her appearance, which was truly unforgettable. Tall, ramrod straight, Mildred Cleghorn was a proud Chiricahua Apache woman whose gray, white, and silver hair framed a dark-skinned face much younger looking than its years. Her voice was soft; she spoke in an articulate way and smiled broadly. She wore huge glasses—sometimes rimless, sometimes not—that hid sad brown eyes. Silver rings and bracelets and white-beaded earrings matched her hair. Wordlessly, Mildred Cleghorn communicated authority and an eloquent physical, emotional, and intellectual supremacy . . . undoubtedly bred in the bone. But she attributed her charisma, when I mentioned it, to something else. "Good genes," she said to me in response to a question, and then added, "Could be the air out here in Oklahoma or the good country food." That certainly might have been true, for she also had energy and vitality to spare and relied on her continuing good health to enable her to travel anywhere at anytime with her dolls or as she represented her people or her church.

I attended one of her lectures in the 1980s at the Laboratory of Anthropology in Santa Fe, New Mexico. Before Mildred talked about her dolls she pulled out a roll of tape and a pair of scissors from an enormous black canvas purse that she lugged along with her everywhere. This was no ordinary lady's pocketbook. It was more like carry-on luggage for travelers and was very heavy. I never discovered what made it so weighty but recall that whenever she was asked for anything—pencils, pens, note paper, maps, extra pairs of glasses, an appointment book, telephone numbers, etc.—she had it in there. So, I was not surprised when the tape and scissors emerged from her purse and she proceeded to hang a map of the United States on the blackboard behind her. Taking a black marker in hand, also retrieved from the pocketbook, she drew a line from southeast Arizona to St. Augustine, Florida, and stopped for a second or two of well-timed silence. Still with her back toward the audience, she then extended the line to Santa Rosa Island, just off the coast of Pensacola. She continued westward to a spot on the map north of Mobile, Alabama, halted for a few seconds, and then with a flourish, drew the last part of the line into southwest Oklahoma. Taking a deep breath, she replaced the cap on the marker and turned toward the gathering. "My people were taken from their homes in the Southwest," she began. Everyone was so quiet that the room sounded empty. Later, when telling me that she always made that unique experience[19] part of her public presentations, she added that she felt obligated to inform audiences all over the country about what "Uncle Sam" had done to the Chiricahuas.

Deliberately to create an opportunity to talk about the history of her tribe and its relations with the United States government, she always brought at least one doll wearing an Apache dress. Along with describing the dresses and cultures expressed by all the dolls with her, she eventually focused on the Chiricahua doll and then, if she had not already done it, she launched into the imprisonment experience. Yet, there was never a note of bitterness in her voice, no sarcasm when she discussed the historical United States policies against the Chiricahuas, and never a sign of animosity toward the government. Occasionally, though, in private conversations a tear or two filled her eyes and after turning her face away for a few seconds, she would finish her comments by talking about "Uncle Sam" not keeping his promises to the Apache people.[20] Her goal, as she told me, was to inform as many people whenever and wherever she could so that the event would never be forgotten. The dolls, beyond their obvious artistic appeal, were her way of accomplishing that purpose.

Mildred's creative talent has been recognized by worldwide collectors and acknowledged by government officials and Native Americans as well. For example, each year the fourteen directors of the American Indian Exposition held in Anadarko, Oklahoma, vote on an individual to become the "Indian of the Year." In 1989 Mildred Cleghorn was chosen to be so honored because of the many varied and significant contributions she made for all Native Americans. Along with public ceremonies and participation in major events associated with the fifty-eighth annual exposition, she received a letter of commendation from the governor of Oklahoma, Henry Bellmon. The governor acknowledged her work at directing the services and activities for her tribe, her continuing participation in community and church activities, and the creation of dolls "which have become recognized nationally for their authenticity and museum quality . . . The State of Oklahoma," wrote the governor, "is proud to join with members of the American Indian Exposition and the 14 participating tribes in honoring you, Mildred Imach Cleghorn, as Outstanding Indian for 1989."[21] And how did that make her feel? "Humble," she said, and then repeated herself very softly. "Humble. I never thought I would be so honored."[22]

That same year the Fort Sill Chiricahua/Warm Springs Apache Tribe celebrated its seventy-fifth anniversary of freedom from incarceration, led, of course, by its chairperson [as she wanted to be called]. Standing alone for just a moment in bright Oklahoma sunshine, Mildred Cleghorn shivered as she wrapped herself in a thick woolen robin's egg blue Pendleton blanket. Pulling the ankle-length wrap up to cover her ears and hair, she hunkered down into the folds. One would think it were December or January, but no, this was September 23, 1989. Unseasonable weather, the result of Hurricane Hugo slamming into the coastline one thousand miles east, brought cold winds blowing more than twenty-five miles an hour across the hills and valleys of the southwestern part of the landlocked state. Less hardy souls sought cover in their vehicles, but Mildred strolled the grounds of the tribal complex, greeted old friends and visitors, smiled pleasantly, and pretended she was warm. Every now and then she sniffled, brought her hand holding a paper tissue out from under the blanket, and blew her nose. Only rarely was she absent from the center of activities and then just for a short period of time. She had much to celebrate and, in true Apache fashion, permitted little to interrupt her plans. After all, she was celebrating not only her tribe's freedom but her own release from incarceration as well. Pulling the blanket a little tighter, she forgot the cold.[23]

The following year, 1990, Mildred was also publicly honored—this time at a major event in Indian country called Red Earth. In June of each year, American Indian festivities known as Red Earth are held in Oklahoma City and are dedicated to the preservation and continued development of Native American culture though a variety of art forms. The huge celebration, started in 1987, brings together craftspeople from more than one hundred tribes, all ready to share the richness and diversity of their heritage with each other and with the world. A colorful pamphlet announcing the gala event states, "Within the Native American runs an artistic spirit as elemental as the sun and stars, and tied to the earth and its resources. The tradition of Indian arts was already thousands of years old when the Spanish explorers trekked across the North American continent in the 1500s. From generation to generation the symbols and their meanings have been passed down. But many arts and crafts forms are as modern as today, drawn from inspirations that link the present with the rich tradition of the past."[24]

This description suits perfectly Mildred's craftwork, and the board of directors responsible for Red Earth thought so, too. They appointed her the "Honored One" for 1990, and as part of the occasion, she rode along a parade route in an open convertible, smiling at bystanders she did not recognize and waving enthusiastically at familiar faces. Ironically, just ahead of her, forty marching members of the Fort Sill 77th Army Band announced her presence by blaring their trumpets and beating their drums. It was a delicious moment for a woman who was born a prisoner of war and whose parents had been under the jurisdiction of the American military at Fort Sill for most of their youth.

Behind Mildred, a breathtaking spectacle filled the streets of Oklahoma City. Wearing feathers of many colors, and the vibrant yellows, reds, tans, oranges, blues, and blacks of tribal costumes Red Earth 1990 paraders marched through the downtown's concrete canyons, keeping time with the pulses of Northern and Southern Plains drums. Hundreds of dancers from diverse tribes stomped the pavement with the cowhide or buckskin soles of their beaded moccasins, tossed their headdresses high, and twisted their torsos in rhythm with the ceaseless beats of the drums. For Mildred Cleghorn, the parade's grand marshal and the event's Honored One, it was a special moment to remember and cherish.[25]

Much later, Red Earth officials presented her with a glass circle anchored to a glass base. Inscribed in the circle are words of respect from her peers: "Red Earth, Inc. designated Mildred Cleghorn Honored One who embraces and embodies the collective wisdom of her cultural experience. June 7, 1990." Criteria for the coveted selection of Honored One also include "the artist's excellence of artistic, creative and technical skills and influence on the Native American community as a whole."[26]

When all of the public honors and activities were finished, Mildred returned home and got ready to go back to work. After a period of absence from her desk, correspondence and other paperwork related to administering a tribe were usually piled high. Undaunted, she went through the papers, page by page, responded to telephone calls noted on pink slips of office memos, dictated letters, did some troubleshooting, made appointments, and addressed all the routine office tasks that needed a leader's touch. Often she worked late into the night and sometimes on weekends, but not on Wednesdays and not on Sundays. Those were church times and she tried never to miss them when she was home.

On one visit to Oklahoma that happened to be on a Wednesday, I was delayed in leaving Albuquerque and arrived at her door just fifteen minutes before church was scheduled to start. Since it was about a five-minute drive to town and the Apache Reformed Church, Mildred had placed all the ingredients of a taco supper out on her counter for me before she left. Having had nothing to eat since breakfast, I was awfully hungry. "Well, we haven't got time to eat now," she said, just as I walked in the door. "You're late and I want you to come to church with me. We sing hymns on Wednesday evenings." Reluctantly I accompanied her, and we stayed in church until 9:30, singing and studying and hearing a sermon. By that time I was famished. Back at Mildred's house, she began putting away the taco makings and said, "Oh, you don't want to eat now. We're going to bed and you'll have bad dreams on a full stomach." There was nothing I could say until I heard her giggle and then knew she was teasing.

As a faithful parishioner, Mildred was an elder in the Reformed Church of America at Apache, Oklahoma, and represented the government of the church at the American Indian Council Committee, a group of six tribes under the umbrella of the church. Also, she sat on the general program council, one of the top organizations within the Reformed Church of America. "I don't want to give the wrong impression," she once told me when we discussed her religion, "but the symbolism we have in the Apache tribe is the same symbolism that Christ has in the Bible. For example, fire. In our way, fire is very important. You notice the fire when we dance, when the *Gah'e* dance around the fire. Well, the Holy Spirit came down to the fire too. Our people went up into the mountains, the high places, and Moses did that. They went up to fast and pray, and they got a message. Moses too got a message. That's why I say it's amazing how our people relate to the biblical standards of the Christian religion, the symbolism. Like the fire and the pollen. You can't get a flower or growth without pollen. Pollen to us represents fertility and we color our clothes with pollen. That's why yellow is such a predominant color among our Apache people. There are so many beautiful things about our Indian people, our Indian way, that I hope we shall never lose. Also, we're taught to share in the Apache way," she added. "Well, there in the book of Matthew it tells you [all about sharing]. The birds and the bees don't worry about what they're going to eat tomorrow, and that's the way our Indian people are. Today is when you live. So, you do what you can today to help other people, to share. I try to live a Christian life, be a good Christian. I study the Bible like you do each day if you're a Christian." In view of that remarkable attitude, I asked her how she felt about what happened to her forebears. "Well, I guess I've accepted it to a certain extent, but then again, I haven't. I still feel a personal loss. I can't speak my language today. I can understand it, yes, but we've lost it here in Oklahoma, and we've lost a lot of the good things." Mentioning other cultural customs that are no longer observed by the Fort Sill Apache tribe's members, Mildred cited the puberty ceremony. Although Dorothy Naiche, the granddaughter of Cochise and the daughter of Naiche, made Mildred's puberty dress, there was no ceremony in which to wear it. "Here in Oklahoma," she said, "we never had them [puberty ceremonies]. We didn't have anyone here to do the ceremony." She lowered her eyes. "I definitely feel I lost something. Definitely. And I don't think it will ever come back. It's gone for good."[27]

In 1996 Mildred made a difficult decision: retirement from her long-standing tribal leadership role. Her health was still good, she was happy and comfortable, and she could still travel and represent her tribe when asked. The twenty years she served as chairperson had passed quickly; she had been reelected ten times during that period.

For two decades, it had been hard to catch her behind her desk but never difficult to find her "on the road." Her staff could always track her. If she was not in Washington, D.C., addressing a congressional committee, she was in Colorado attending and speaking at a Native American Rights Fund meeting. If not there, she was in California, accepting an honor. If not there . . . somewhere else.

Throughout her productive life Mildred Cleghorn was also publicly recognized for her many achievements on behalf of her tribe. Always reluctant to talk about herself, I coaxed information about two accomplishments that meant a great deal. During her tenure in office the tribe acquired acreage contiguous to the existing landholdings, which is an extremely significant environmental and psychological accomplishment for a group of Native Americans whose ancestors were originally land based. Mildred was also responsible for negotiating with Richard Shaw, an Arizonan whose family held title to certain land in the Cochise Stronghold. Mr. Shaw returned four acres of his property to the Oklahoma Chiricahuas and was the special invited guest at a function in the Stronghold when the land was transferred.

Other successes were also quite worthy. Back home in Apache, Mildred was the overseer of government grant moneys that enabled one large building containing a gymnasium and new offices to be added to the tribal complex of offices, a smoke shop, out buildings, and dance grounds. While she was chairperson, social programs such as child care, housing, and an emergency youth shelter were instituted. She became instrumental in keeping an Indian Hospital in Lawton open, even testifying before Congress on the situation. And on and on.

Sadly, her life ended too soon. News of her tragic and violent death in an automobile accident near her home on the morning of April 15, 1997, echoed across Indian country, from coast to coast, in a matter of hours. Paul Harvey, the radio commentator, picked up the news from the Associated Press and put it on the air immediately. Newspapers printed the item in their late editions. By the next morning, Indians and non-Indians alike, most everyone whom Mildred had touched in some way—and others as well—were aware that this Chiricahua Apache woman had gone on. She had become "a legend in her own time" as the saying goes, and at her death a particular page of American and Native American history had been turned.

During one of several invited eulogies at the Apache Reformed Church, an eloquent orator from the Mescalero Apache Reservation likened Mildred to Lozen. He said that both women were outstanding leaders, paused, and then quickly moved on in his tribute to say that both women were revered by their people. Mildred would have gasped at even the thought of being mentioned in the same breath as Lozen, and would have certainly uttered one of her favorite lines, "Oh, my conscience!"

Later that morning an orderly and silent funeral procession left the Fort Sill Chiricahua/Warm Springs Apache gymnasium. The long, long line of cars with lights on, led by a hearse, moved slowly along the road to Lawton, past the bend in the road where her brick house stands with its large living room windows facing the east. Just past the house, cars on the other side of the two-lane road pulled over in respect. Reaching the highway into Lawton, we drove for only a short distance toward Fort Sill. Here too cars stopped on the other side of the four lanes. Traveling down a ramp onto the military reserve, the cortege passed the flat field that was Noche's village where a little girl once romped and played with her cousin. The procession wound around all the twists and turns of the roads that lead to the Apache prisoner of war cemetery. At each bend along the way white-gloved military men in uniforms stood at attention and saluted this Chiricahua Apache chief. Other soldiers and Army officers were at the gravesite in the Apache prisoner-of-war cemetery, just a few feet from where Go-lah-at-tsa was buried in 1902, and not far from the final resting place of Geronimo. Mildred's casket stayed above ground for a few minutes, covered with the blue Pendleton blanket that had warmed her many years ago, a shawl, and an American flag. The minister spoke, a bugler blared "Taps," and then the soldiers carefully removed the flag, folded it, and gave it to her grandson. Her coffin was slowly lowered and many of us relatives and friends threw a handful of the Oklahoma earth she loved so much onto the casket. We remained for a while at the gravesite, talking softly and singing in English and Apache, and then returned in our private cars to the tribal complex. On the drive back to Apache I remembered that Mildred had told me her wish was to be an Apache throughout eternity. No doubt it had now been granted.

In quiet conversations during the next few hours I learned that the Army wanted to salute her at the grave with their guns. Her family declined, stating that they thought the Chiricahuas had had enough experiences with the Army's weapons and did not want any more. I believe Mildred would have agreed.

NOTES

INTRODUCTION

1. Eve Ball's book, *Indeh,* remains one of the classics of all the books about the Chiricahua Apaches. She told me more than twenty years ago about the great difficulty she had in getting that work published. She faced incredible obstacles because she was a woman writing about the Chiricahuas, and publishers raised their eyebrows at that. Another impediment was that publishers were not certain there was a market for a book about the Chiricahuas and consequently were reluctant to commit the resources necessary to publish her work. At long last, Brigham Young University Press in Provo, Utah, took a chance and came up with a winner. Eve Ball was my mentor and I spent many hours in her Ruidoso, New Mexico, home listening to her respond to my questions about herself and her work with the Chiricahuas. When she died in December, 1984, and was buried from St. Joseph's Mission Church on the Mescalero Apache Reservation, I decided to become more active in my relations with the Apaches. Although no one will ever fill Eve's shoes, if she were still here I hope she would be happy with my work.

2. Asa Daklugie's father was Chief Juh of the Nedni Apaches and "the epitome of an Apache warrior," according to Dan L. Thrapp in his biography of Juh. Entitled *Juh: An Incredible Indian,* this work too has become a classic. I am fortunate in that during the last decade or so the late Dan Thrapp honored me by guiding my research into unexplored areas of Chiricahua Apache history and culture and by inspiring me to persevere despite encountering obstacles dissimilar to Eve Ball's circumstances but frustrating nonetheless. Eugene Chihuahua's father was Chief Chihuahua of the Chiricahuas; he was not as well known as some of the other Apache leaders but was prominent among his people. Chihuahua and his band surrendered six months before Geronimo, probably because Chihuahua was able to ascertain the risks of remaining in the field and on the run from the U.S. Army. In that regard, it could be said that he was a wise man and saved the lives of many members of his band. On the other hand, perhaps some of those Apaches, after three decades of imprisonment, would have rather died fighting. Both Asa Daklugie and Eugene Chihuahua became leaders of the Chiricahuas when they were finally freed and living on the Mescalero Apache Reservation and talking with Eve Ball.

3. For more information, see H. Henrietta Stockel, *Survival of the Spirit.* This book describes the years of imprisonment and all of the experiences and ramifications in great detail.

CHAPTER 1. BEGINNINGS

1. For two more examples of Apache creation myths, see Morris E. Opler, *Myths and Tales,* and John G. Bourke, "Notes on Apache Mythology."
2. Perrone, et al., *Medicine Women,* pp. 9–10.
3. Anna Birgitta Rooth, "The Creation Myths of the North American Indians," p. 503. Rooth concludes that the small number (eight) of categories are related to the tribes' geography. She believes there is a connection between Asiatic and American creation myths, and, if she is correct, that affiliation supports the beliefs about early groups, including the Chiricahua Apaches, crossing the Bering Strait from Asia into Alaska.
4. Opler, "The Concept of Supernatural Power," p. 66. Opler's article addresses "power," among the Chiricahua Apaches, a major feature of their religion.
5. Opler, *Myths and Tales,* p. xiii.
6. Opler, *An Apache Life-Way,* p. 197.
7. This tale of destruction of the old world was recorded by Opler in *Myths and Tales,* p. 1. It is only one explanation of how the world began and seems to reflect Christian influence. Opler believes that if there was a flood story before white contact, it has been altered. On page 1 in a footnote, Opler quotes a Chiricahua as saying, "There was a world before this one according to the old Indians and it was destroyed by water. All the people living before this world were washed out."
8. Harry Hoijer, *Chiricahua and Mescalero Apache Texts,* p. 13.
9. S. M. Barrett, *Geronimo,* pp. 59–64.
10. Opler, *An Apache Life-Way,* pp. 196–97.
11. Ball, *In the Days of Victorio,* pp. 68–70. There are many versions of this tale.
12. Opler, *Myths and Tales,* pp. 14–15. For a detailed description of a Western Apache puberty ceremony, see Keith Basso, "The Gift of Changing Woman."
13. The dancers imitate the true *Gah'e,* a race of supernatural beings, according to Chiricahua legend, who live in the mountains. They function mostly to cure disease and are considered particularly effective in driving away epidemics. See Opler, *Myths and Tales,* pp. 74–78. The dancers are endowed with the full powers of the gods they impersonate. Every mark, bell, and symbol on their costumes has its own meaning and "represents something from heaven, from the earth or from beneath the ground. It is taboo for anyone to recognize the impersonators as men they know." (J. Wesley Huff, "The Mountain Spirits Dance at Gallup.") For a detailed explanation of the Mountain Spirits, see also Opler, "Mountain Spirits of the Chiricahua Apache."
14. Stockel, *Survival of the Spirit,* p. 90.
15. Berle Kanseah, conversation with author, Oct. 9, 1993.

1. This has recently been the subject of some dispute by non-Apache writers, but is part of the tribe's oral history.
2. Federal Writers Project, "The Apache," pp. 8–10.
3. Stockel, "Swatches Tu Moonwalker," p. 24, and Stockel, "By Hands So Deft," pp. 64–67.
4. Also called "agave," a perennial plant growing in arid and semiarid regions of American. The broad, linear, fibrous leaves grow upward from next to the ground to form a massive rosette. They are gray and smooth on both sides and have prickly edges. After ten years or more, the plant produces a flower stalk twenty to forty feet tall that bears large, yellowish-green flowers on many horizontal branches. The fruit is a three-celled capsule. After flowering and fruiting, the plant ordinarily dies, but that is not always the case.
5. Rattlesnakes are quite common in Apacheria, as are Arizona coral snakes, and varieties of rear-fanged snakes. Although scorpions are reputed to be among the deadliest inhabitants of desert regions, the sting of only the bark scorpion is regarded as dangerous. Giant centipedes average about eight inches in length but can be as long as twelve inches. They have an average of twenty body segments, each with a pair of legs. The tarantula is the largest spider in southwest deserts. Adults vary in size and have dense hair on the abdomen and legs. They live in burrows where they stay during the day and venture out at night for food. Black widow spiders rarely leave their webs, which are found in crevices, rodent burrows, and rock and debris piles. Their venom is a neuro-muscular toxin. More dangerous, however, is the brown recluse spider whose venom is composed of enzymes that can cause tissue breakdowns. Within twelve hours to several days a narcotic lesion resembling a bull's eye forms that can take months to heal. Brown recluse spiders also spin webs and normally reside under logs, rocks, debris, in pack rat nests, and other similar habitats.
6. According to George H. LaBerge, M.D., writing in *Arizona Highways,* "Sage was well known to the Indians, who used it for seasoning, as poultices for sprains (in which it is very effective), for bronchial troubles and diarrhea."
7. Escoba de Vibora is still used today as a treatment for arthritis, rheumatism, and sore muscles, but it is placed in hot bath water, not taken as a tea. "It is common, safe, and may sometimes work so well for joint inflammations as to supplant salicylate (aspirin) treatment or be used alternately with other pharmaceutical drugs to decrease their side effects." (Michael Moore, *Medicinal Plants,* p. 56.) In a later publication, *Los Remedios,* Moore states that the primary use of Escoba de Vibora is for "arthritis" when a "small bundle of the dried tops is steeped in a pot of hot water, a small amount is drunk, and the rest added to a tub of bathwater for a soak" (p. 42).
8. Opler, *An Apache Life-Way,* p. 410.
9. Angie Debo, *Geronimo,* pp. 225, 234–35. Unfaithfulness was not always punished in this manner. One of the myths and tales recorded by Opler (*Myths and Tales,* p. 87) tells of a woman whose husband suspected her of infidelity.

He said to her, "You are going to dance naked before all the camp or I am going to kill you."

10. Opler, *An Apache Life-Way,* p. 411.

11. Robert S. Ove and H. Henrietta Stockel, *Geronimo's Kids,* pp. 68–70.

12. Opler, *An Apache Life-Way,* p. 402.

13. Debo, *Geronimo,* 469n.

14. An old cooked agave heart was recently found in the Dragoon Mountains of southern Arizona by a team of archeologists. The heart was charred on one side and indented where it had been burned in the fire. The leaves appeared to have been cut off and dried sap that ran during the cooking process was still present on some of the outer leaves. The arid desert climate had apparently preserved the agave heart for more than a century.

15. Kinship among Chiricahuas is different from the surrounding society's reckoning. In the Apache way, kinship is counted bilaterally, through the mother and father equally. Four terms are used to express the parent-child relationship, but the terms for father and mother are like no others. The maternal aunt and uncle are very important to the child as are the individuals called "cousins" by the dominant society. These are akin to "brother" and "sister" in the dominant society. The relations between a child and his mother's brother and brother's wife are somewhat different due to the custom of matrilocal residence. The child's uncle will be in the immediate family only until he marries and then joins his wife's residence. Nonetheless, he will pay particular attention to his sister's son, the nephew, and have a hand in teaching the boy the ways of Apache men. A child's mother's siblings are all addressed by one kinship term, which is also used to address a mother's cousins and any female cousin's child. One kinship term is also used to address a child's father's brother and father's sister and includes the father's male and female cousins as well. It also designates a brother's child and a male cousin's child. And it gets even more complicated. For detailed descriptions of kinship terms and a kinship system map, see Opler, *An Apache Life-Way.* Ishton might have been Geronimo's cousin or another close relative, but she was not his "sister" as the term is understood in the Anglo culture. However, their relationship was so close in life that she is buried only a few feet from him in the Chiricahua Apache prisoner-of-war cemetery at Fort Sill, Oklahoma.

16. Ball, *Indeh,* p. 8.

17. Mildred Cleghorn, interview with author, Aug. 8, 1989.

18. Awls were used by the Chiricahuas for many purposes that called for the use of hides. Cases used for carrying awls were also made from hides and often decorated with beads or jingles. This type of craftwork continued during incarceration, but unfortunately, few items from Chiricahua material culture remain today. Most articles that have survived are individually owned by Apache families, although a few are exhibited at the Mescalero Apache Cultural Center on the Mescalero Apache Reservation in New Mexico.

19. Jose Cortes, *Views from the Apache Frontier,* p. 59.

1. Stockel, *Women of the Apache Nation,* p. 25.
2. James L. Haley, *Apaches: A History and Culture Portrait,* p. 123.
3. Also called antelope sage and, according to Vogel, in *American Indian Medicine,* p. 243, it was also boiled and drunk by women during menstruation to prevent conception.
4. When people died, their names were not spoken again for fear that their ghosts would hear the names and return to earth to haunt the speaker. When mentioning the deceased, synonyms and circumlocutions were often used. For example, if a dead woman's name was "Rainbow," talking about her would require saying something like, "I recall that woman whose name was like that multicolored arc in the sky that appears after a rain."
5. Opler, *An Apache Life-Way,* p. 12.
6. Carol S. Wolman, M.D., "The Cradleboard of the Western Indians," p. 306.
7. Some years ago I found a cradleboard's frame made of strong wire. It had been discarded for one reason or another, and, upon bringing it to the attention of a few Chiricahua women, I was advised to take it back where I found it and leave it there. They were extremely uncomfortable with the fact that I had removed it from the ground in front of an old abandoned house.
8. John Upton Terrell, *Apache Chronicle,* p. 93.
9. Ove and Stockel, *Geronimo's Kids,* p. 83.
10. Opler, *Myths and Tales,* p. 41.
11. Ibid., p. 23.
12. Note the similarity between this tale and the creation myth told by Geronimo.
13. Opler, *An Apache Life-Way,* p. 27.
14. Stockel, *Women of the Apache Nation,* p. 130.
15. Ibid., pp. 30–31.
16. A small number of children, possibly eight, were sent to the Hampton Normal and Industrial Institute in Hampton, Virginia. Opened in April, 1868, Hampton was established for blacks and was partly funded by the American Missionary Association. I have been unable to discover the selection process used to choose which Apache children would attend Hampton.
17. This reference to the Sisters of Charity may be incorrect. I believe the Order was the Sisters of St. Joseph.
18. U.S. Senate Executive Document 73, vol. 2448, 49th Cong., 2nd sess. As with most numbers compiled and kept by government sources of that time, the figures are disputable. For example, the Carlisle Indian School has now identified 269 Apache students *from all Apache bands* who attended their training institution during the years 1879–1918. Of these, my estimate is that more than 112 were Chiricahuas, although my numbers may be low.
19. Sister Mary Albert, conversation with author, July 5, 1991. It should always be remembered that points of view are unique and vary with individuals. It certainly is possible that the Apache children had the wonderful time

described by Sister Mary Albert, but one wonders if the parents of these children saw the experience the same way.

20. Stockel, *Survival of the Spirit*, pp. 116–17.

21. Ibid., pp. 117–18.

22. *Carlisle Indian School Catalog, 1912*, p. 10.

23. Ball, *In the Days of Victorio*, pp. 199–200. James Kaywaykla, son of the warrior woman Gouyen, was nine years old when he was sent to the Carlisle school. In later years he married Dorothy Naiche, daughter of the famous chief and granddaughter of Cochise. As a ten-year-old, Dorothy had arrived with her mother, E-clah-heh, one of Naiche's wives, at Fort Marion. They were part of Chihuahua's group, the first to be incarcerated about six months before Geronimo's final surrender. The Kaywaykla descendants live today in or near Apache, Oklahoma. Debo reported (*Geronimo*, p. 318) that one of the officers said the separation of the children from their confused and frightened families was the most disagreeable task he had ever performed. Desperate mothers hid their smaller children under their skirts.

24. For detailed descriptions of Carlisle's outing program, see David Wallace Adams, *Education for Extinction*, pp. 54, 155–56, 157–63; Stockel, *Survival of the Spirit*, pp. 113–36; Robert A. Trennert, "Educating Indian Girls," pp. 271–90; and Trennert, "From Carlisle to Phoenix," pp. 267–91. While theoretically workable, the outing program could easily be abused by taking advantage of the participants. Eventually this happened in the West, and the program had to be discontinued. (See Stockel, *Survival of the Spirit*, pp. 119–20.)

25. Trennert, "From Carlisle to Phoenix," p. 267.

26. Tuberculosis, for example, was rampant among the general population at the time. When imprisoned, the Chiricahuas had only had limited exposure to the surrounding culture's communicable diseases and thus were "sitting ducks" for the ailments. At Carlisle, the Apache students lived among youngsters from many other tribes, nearly all of whom had some degree of immunity. Nonetheless, they carried the deadly germs and transmitted them through use of common towels, coughing, etc. This circumstance was exacerbated when the Apache students participated in the outing program and became exposed even further when living with families whose members were tubercular. I have compiled the names of thirty-seven Chiricahua children who perished at Carlisle, mainly from tuberculosis (Stockel, *Survival of the Spirit*, pp. 133–34).

27. Shapard Papers, Pratt to Commissioner of Indian Affairs, May 24, 1889. There is no evidence that his statement was taken seriously. Also, his statement about "sifting" the Chiricahuas and the "unhealthy ones disposed of" is chilling and reminiscent of attitudes of those responsible for the Holocaust in Europe not so long ago.

CHAPTER 4. THE PUBERTY CEREMONY

1. Opler, "An Outline of Chiricahua Apache Social Organization," p. 228.
2. Tradition dictates that if the girl has a pleasant attitude during the ceremony, she will have a good disposition for the rest of her life. Whether or not this is true is totally dependent on the personality of the young woman and the events of her life. However, several Chiricahua elders today believe, in looking back over their lives, that this section of the puberty ceremony had a beneficial influence on them and was a determining factor in how they lived their adult lives.
3. A more detailed description of this entire ceremony is in Claire R. Farrer's book, *Living Life's Circle: Mescalero Apache Cosmovision*. Although quite technical, this book approaches the ceremony from an ethnoastronomy perspective, but it contains valuable information about several other beliefs as well. If you are thinking of reading it, be prepared to spend time with the book. In correspondence, Karl H. Schlesier, author of the historical novel, *Josanie's War*, wrote, "Much more than a puberty rite, the *gotal* (the Chiricahua term for it) was a new life ceremony, a ceremony of regeneration of the natural world through the medium of the pubescent girl. During the ceremony the girl was ritually transformed into White Painted Woman. With her, through the singer's (Thunder) sacred songs, the natural world was once again made new and plentiful as it had been in the beginning of Chiricahua time. The lodge essentially was a spirit lodge from which the miracle of transformation was enacted." (Letter to author and Texas A&M University Press dated Mar. 2, 1999.)
4. Ball, *Indeh*, p. 58.
5. Opler, *An Apache Life-Way*, p. 109.
6. Ibid., p. 110.

CHAPTER 5. YESTERDAY'S WARRIOR WOMEN

1. Warrior women were so designated not only because they fought beside the men in battle—which some did—but also because they did something considered to be "exceptional."
2. The Warm Springs Apaches are a band of the Chiricahua Apaches. Classification of the Chiricahuas into bands has become somewhat confusing because of the varying viewpoints of anthropologists and historians as to what constitutes a "grouping." Whatever they decide, I prefer to believe in James Kaywakla's statement to Eve Ball (Ball, *In the Days of Victorio*, p. xiv), e.g., that in historical times there were only two true bands of Chiricahuas: the Warm Springs, and the Chiricahuas themselves. Other bands important to these two Chiricahua groups were the Nedni and the Bedonkohe. Geronimo was born into the Bedonkohe band but at the time of surrender was with Cochise's son Naiche in the Chiricahua band as was the Warm Springs Apache Lozen. Time and the weapons of two countries—Mexico and the United

States—had reduced the other bands so much in size that over a period of years the survivors had to join the remaining band, the Chiricahuas, for safety and sustenance.

3. Dan L. Thrapp has written eloquently and thoroughly about this battle and all of Victorio's life in his classic work, *Victorio and the Mimbres Apaches.*

4. This flight to safety has been described in great detail by Eve Ball in *In the Days of Victorio,* pp. 168–74.

5. Ken Bonnell, letter to author, Jan. 19, 1994.

6. Elbys Hugar, interview with author, May 8, 1989.

7. The details of this remarkable feat are found in Ball, *Indeh,* pp. 204–10. Questions have arisen regarding the role of the Comanches in this story. Comanches were ostensibly on the reservation at the time (1879) and thus should have been unable to enter into fights with other tribes. Comanche oral history, however, reports that reservation life was not as restricted as once thought. Young men often raided into Mexico from Texas and could have ridden into New Mexico and committed raids upon other tribes as well. As for the buckskin dress, Gouyen had worn it twice previously—once at her puberty ceremony and the next time at her wedding to the young man who was killed.

8. James Kaywaykla was one of the Apache men who spoke at length with Eve Ball and whose memories of life in freedom were recorded by her in *Indeh* and in *In the Days of Victorio.*

9. Although Eliza Coonie has usually been called Dahteste's "niece," she was actually the daughter of Dahteste's husband Coonie and his first wife. Thus, Eliza was actually Dahteste's stepdaughter.

10. Ball and Lynda A. Sanchez, "Legendary Apache Women," pp. 11–12.

11. Hugar, interview with author, May 8, 1989.

12. Ove, correspondence with author, Dec., 1995. Dahteste was a member of the Dutch Reformed Church at Whitetail and participated in the ladies' auxiliary activities. In order to do so, she must have understood English but still refused to speak the language. Dahteste is buried in the church cemetery at Whitetail, which is now overgrown. Most graves are unmarked and the cemetery plat was destroyed in a fire, I am told. Consequently, the actual burial sites of many Whitetail residents cannot be determined, and the families cannot visit or tend the graves by clearing out the growth that continues to cover the cemetery ground.

13. This is the generally accepted approximate date of Lozen's birth but is still speculation. Victorio was born around 1825, making him about twenty years older than Lozen.

14. Said by Dan L. Thrapp to have "some claim to the title of America's greatest guerilla fighter," Victorio became chief of the Warm Springs Apaches. Lozen fought with him, side by side, until October 15, 1880, when a group of Mexican irregulars, commissioned by Chihuahua's governor, Luis Terrazas, laid an ambush for Victorio's band and killed seventy-eight, including the chief. Sixty-eight women and children were taken prisoner and subsequently

marched into the heart of Mexico where few were heard from again. (Thrapp, *Encyclopedia of Frontier Biography*, III, pp. 1483–85.) Lozen and a number of other warriors were not present at Victorio's encampment on the day the massacre took place. Immediately afterward, she and Chief Loco led a retaliatory strike across northern Mexico, southeastern Arizona, and southwestern New Mexico.

15. Ball, *In the Days of Victorio*, p. 14. Outside interest in Lozen waxes and wanes. Periodically I experience intense interest via letters and e-mail asking many questions about her, and then it abates for a while. Lozen seems to have captured the imagination of many readers, many of whom insist there is more information about her that is being deliberately withheld from the public's eyes. All are welcome to research the topic, but, unfortunately, I cannot add anymore to what has already been printed.

16. In surrender negotiations, General George Crook said to Geronimo, "You must make up your own mind whether you will stay out on the warpath or surrender unconditionally. If you stay out, I'll keep after you and kill the last one, if it takes fifty years." (Debo, *Geronimo*, p. 259.) Geronimo believed him, and, according to Mildred Cleghorn [in a conversation with me several years ago], "Geronimo didn't want the name 'Apache' to die and so he agreed to give up."

17. It was not an all-or-nothing situation among the Apaches. Warriors who did not choose to surrender with Geronimo were free to leave the campsite and go their own way, at least according to Chiricahua custom. It is a sure bet that the American military officials did not like this tradition. Nonetheless, this effort at surrender failed, because the warriors became drunk and fled the scene. The final capitulation occurred about six months later.

18. I have attempted to find the sites said to be burial grounds at Mount Vernon, Alabama, but either the land is overgrown with wild brush or I have been misled. I have been told by officials at the prison site (now a mental institution) that they do not have any records of where the deceased prisoners were buried because the Apaches buried their dead in unmarked graves in a field. That is as difficult for me to believe as the information I received later from the Dutch Reformed Church, e.g., that they have no record of who is buried where at the Whitetail cemetery because the information burned in a fire. It seems to me that records of deaths and disposal of remains of these Chiricahua prisoners of war would have been meticulously kept, given the notoriety of the prisoners.

CHAPTER 6. TODAY'S WARRIOR WOMAN: MILDRED IMACH CLEGHORN

1. George Wratten had grown up with the Apaches at the San Carlos, Arizona, agency where his father was employed. He spoke the language fluently, and, as a civilian employee of the Army, he had accompanied Lieutenant Charles B. Gatewood and his troops into Mexico in pursuit of the Chiricahuas. After

Geronimo's surrender, Wratten remained with the Apaches. He traveled with the captive warriors from their homelands in the Southwest to Fort Pickens, Florida, where seventeen of the men were first imprisoned. When, nearly one year later, they were transferred to Alabama and joined their families, George continued to live and work among the prisoners. Little is known about Annie, except that she was related to Lot Eyelash, one of Geronimo's warriors and that she had been orphaned as a youngster while imprisoned in Alabama. Amy's younger sister, Blossom, later became the wife of Sam Haozous and the mother of five children, one of whom was noted sculptor Allan Houser. The girls lived with their parents until Wratten's mother visited the prison camp in Alabama. Soon after she left to return home, Annie and George divorced, and she remarried. Believing he was unable to care for his daughters, Wratten turned the young girls over to Joh-nstah [called Ben Francis by the Army] and his wife Nah-tai-che who raised them. A few years later Wratten married Bessie Cannon, a local young woman. They had five children, none of whom apparently had any contact with the half-sisters until Albert Wratten, as an adult, traveled to Apache, Oklahoma, and knocked on the door of the Haozous home. "You Blossom?" he asked when a woman opened the door. From that time until today the family has stayed in touch. Annie subsequently married Talbot Gooday, a Chiricahua prisoner, and, after a long marriage and many children, died on January 17, 1913, of extensive capillary embolism, the result of severe burns she received from an accident in the prison camp at Fort Sill.

2. Two schools of thought exist regarding those Apaches who were designated to remain in Oklahoma. One believes that the Army chose the "educated" young men and women because there were no reservations in Oklahoma and further assimilation and acculturation would occur quickly. The other belief is that some Apaches volunteered to remain in the state while others opted for New Mexico and that the Army respected their choices.

3. At the time of its creation in 1901, each of the 326.7 acres comprising the town sold for $1.25 each. Mildred told me that the Apache prisoners had been promised 160 acres each upon release, but "No one got 160 acres. The closest they got was 158 acres and the least amount they got was 23. A majority received 80 acres apiece. My father got 80 acres, my mother got 80 acres, and I live right here on my 50 acres. Yes, we were promised 160 acres apiece, but Uncle Sam doesn't follow through. [Even though we were released in 1914], it was about 1923 [when] the last Apache got an allotment. I'm still fighting. We have a good way. The quality of life the old folks lived when free was beautiful. It was loving and sharing, and what else can you ask? Too bad that's not the white man's way. Most of our Indian people have extended families clear down to the umpteenth cousin, you might say. You're still my relative, you still have the same blood I have. It might be a drop, but it's still there. And I'll share all I have with you."

4. Blossom W. Haozous, interview with Pat O'Brien, July 22, 1976.

5. Ibid.

6. Cleghorn, interviews with author, June, 1990, and Apr., 1992.

7. Cleghorn, lecture, Oct. 10, 1992.

8. Cleghorn, interview, May 5, 1992.

9. Ibid., Aug. 8, 1989.

10. Ibid., May 5, 1992.

11. Cleghorn, interview with author, June, 1990.

12. As prisoners, the Chiricahua Apaches ran cows at Fort Sill and sold the entire herd prior to being freed. Proceeds from the sale were divided among the families, and it is with these moneys that they were able to purchase houses and other structures already on the land they would be allotted.

13. *Lawton Constitution-Morning Press,* Oct. 5, 1969.

14. Stockel, "Tribal Distinctions," p. 99.

15. Cleghorn, interviews with author, June 6, 1990, and May 5, 1992.

16. Ibid., May 4, 1986.

17. Ibid., June 6, 1990.

18. Ibid., May 5, 1992.

19. No other tribe in American history was similarly treated.

20. Stockel, *Women of the Apache Nation,* p. 125.

21. Henry Bellmon, letter to Cleghorn, Aug. 30, 1989. I discussed this letter with Mildred, and she shrugged it off. I got the impression that Governor Bellmon was not one of her favorite politicians.

22. Stockel, *Women of the Apache Nation,* p. 143.

23. This is the same blue blanket that covered her casket in April of 1997.

24. *Red Earth,* pamphlet, 1993.

25. Parades were not new to Mildred Cleghorn. In 1989 on horseback she led the Rose Bowl Parade in Pasadena, California. She usually marched in the American Indian Exposition parades in Anadarko, Oklahoma, in early August of each year. Ordinarily the elders rode in open cars, but Mildred insisted on walking, even during the 1989 parade when she had been designated "Indian of the Year."

26. *Apache [Oklahoma] News,* June 7, 1990.

27. Stockel, *Women of the Apache Nation,* pp. 137–38, 140–41.

BIBLIOGRAPHY

COLLECTIONS

Shapard Papers, Searcy Hospital, Mount Vernon, Alabama.

BOOKS AND ARTICLES

Adams, David Wallace. *Education for Extinction: American Indians and the Boarding School Experience 1875–1928.* Lawrence: University Press of Kansas, 1995.

Ball, Eve. *Indeh: An Apache Odyssey.* Provo: Brigham Young University Press, 1980.

———. "Interpreter for the Apaches." *True West,* November–December, 1971, pp. 26–27, 36.

———. *In the Days of Victorio: Recollections of a Warm Springs Apache.* Tucson: University of Arizona Press, 1970.

——— and Lynda A. Sanchez. "Legendary Apache Women." *Frontier Times,* October–November, 1980, pp. 8–12.

Barrett, S. M. *Geronimo: His Own Story.* New York: Ballantine Books, 1970.

Basso, Keith. "The Gift of Changing Woman." *Bureau of American Ethnology Bulletin* 196, Anthropology Papers No. 76, 1966.

Bourke, John G. "Notes on Apache Mythology." *Journal of American Folklore* 3 (April–June, 1890).

Cortes, Jose. *Views from the Apache Frontier: Report on the Northern Provinces of New Spain.* Edited by Elizabeth A. H. John. Translated by John Wheat. Norman: University of Oklahoma Press, 1989.

Debo, Angie. *Geronimo: The Man, His Time, His Place.* Norman: University of Oklahoma Press, 1976.

Farrer, Claire R. *Living Life's Circle: Mescalero Apache Cosmovision.* Albuquerque: University of New Mexico Press, 1991.

Federal Writers Project. "The Apache." *Arizona State Teachers College Bulletin* 20 (August, 1939).

Haley, James L. *Apaches: A History and Culture Portrait.* Garden City, N.Y.: Doubleday and Company, 1981.

Hoijer, Harry. *Chiricahua and Mescalero Apache Texts with Ethnological Notes by Morris E. Opler.* Chicago: University of Chicago Press, 1938.

Huff, J. Wesley. "The Mountain Spirits Dance at Gallup." *New Mexico Magazine,* July, 1948.

LaBerge, George H., M.D. "The Medicinal Plants of Arizona." *Arizona High-ways*, February, 1933.

Moore, Michael. *Los Remedios: Traditional Herbal Remedies of the Southwest.* Santa Fe: Red Crane Press, 1990.

———. *Medicinal Plants of the Desert and Canyon West.* Santa Fe: Museum of New Mexico Press, 1989.

Opler, Morris E. *An Apache Life-Way. The Economic, Social, & Religious Institutions of the Chiricahua Indians.* Lincoln: University of Nebraska Press, 1996.

———. "Concept of Supernatural Power among the Chiricahua and Mescalero Apaches." American Anthropologist 37:1 (January–March, 1935): 65–70.

———. "Mountain Spirits of the Chiricahua Apache." *The Masterkey,* 20 (1946): 125–31.

———. *Myths and Tales of the Chiricahua Apache Indians.* Lincoln: University of Nebraska Press, 1994.

———. "An Outline of Chiricahua Apache Social Organization." In Eggan, Fred, et al. *Social Anthropology of North American Tribes.* Chicago: University of Chicago Press, 1955, pp. 172–239.

Ove, Robert S. and H. Henrietta Stockel. *Geronimo's Kids: A Teacher's Lessons on the Apache Reservation.* College Station: Texas A&M University Press, 1997.

Perrone, Bobette; H. Henrietta Stockel; and Victoria Krueger. *Medicine Women, Curanderas, and Women Doctors.* Norman: University of Oklahoma Press, 1989.

Rooth, Anna Birgitta. "The Creation Myths of the North American Indians." *Anthropos* 52 (1957): 497–508.

Stockel, H. Henrietta. "By Hands So Deft." *Americana* 17 (July–August, 1989): 64–67.

———. "Farewell Mildred Imach Cleghorn." *Oklahoma Today,* February–March, 1998, pp. 72–74.

———. "In Her Image. Chiricahua Apache Dollmaker Shares Her Heritage." *Southwest Sampler,* spring, 1991, pp. 51–52.

———. *Survival of the Spirit: Chiricahua Apaches in Captivity.* Reno: University of Nevada Press, 1993.

———. "Swatches: Tu Moonwalker Creating Miniature Apache Baskets." *Fiberarts* 19 (summer, 1992): 24.

———. "Tribal Distinctions: Mildred Imach Cleghorn's Dolls Display the Traditional Costumes Worn by Women of Various Indian Tribes." *Dolls: The Collector's Magazine,* July, 1991, pp. 97–99.

———. "Two Women of the Chiricahua." *Native Peoples Magazine,* spring, 1994, pp. 68–71.

———. *Women of the Apache Nation: Voices of Truth.* Reno: University of Nevada Press, 1991.

Thrapp, Dan L. *Juh: An Incredible Indian.* El Paso: Texas Western Press, 1973.

———. *Encyclopedia of Frontier Biography,* III. Lincoln: University of Nebraska

Press in association with The Arthur H. Clark Company, Spokane, Wash., 1988.

————. *Victorio and the Mimbres Apaches.* Norman: University of Oklahoma Press, 1974.

Trennert, Robert A. "Educating Indian Girls at Nonreservation Boarding Schools, 1878–1920." *Western Historical Quarterly* 13:3 (July, 1982).

————. From Carlisle to Phoenix: The Rise and Fall of the Indian Outing System, 1878–1930." *Pacific Historical Review* 52:3 (August, 1983).

Vogel, Virgil J. *American Indian Medicine.* Norman: University of Oklahoma Press, 1970.

Wolman, Carol S., M.D. "The Cradleboard of the Western Indians: A Baby-Tending Device of Cultural Importance." *Clinical Pediatrics* 9 (May, 1970).

INTERVIEWS, CORRESPONDENCE, AND UNPUBLISHED MANUSCRIPTS

Albert, Sister Mary. Telephone conversation with H. Henrietta Stockel, July 5, 1991.

Bellmon, Henry, governor of Oklahoma. Letter to Mildred Imach Cleghorn, chairwoman, Fort Sill Apache Tribe, August 30, 1989.

Bonnell, Ken. Letter to H. Henrietta Stockel, January 19, 1994.

Cleghorn, Mildred. Interviews with H. Henrietta Stockel, August 8, 1989; June 6, 1990; and May 5, 1992.

Griswold, Gillett. "The Fort Sill Apaches: Their Vital Statistics, Tribal Origins, Antecedents." U.S. Army and Missile Center Museum Archives. Fort Sill, Oklahoma, 1970.

Haozous, Blossom W. Interview with Pat O'Brien, July 22, 1976. Bicentennial Oral History Program for the U.S. Army Field Artillery and Fort Sill Museum, Fort Sill, Oklahoma.

Hugar, Elbys. Interview with H. Henrietta Stockel, May 8, 1989.

Ove, Robert S. Letter to H. Henrietta Stockel, December, 1995.

Stockel, H. Henrietta. "Chiricahua Apache Mildred Cleghorn's Dolls: Sugar 'n Spice and Unbleached Muslin . . . ," 1991.

NEWSPAPERS, CATALOGS, AND PAMPHLETS

Lawton [Oklahoma] Constitution-Morning Press, October 5, 1969, and May 4, 1986.

Carlisle Indian School Catalog, 1912.

Red Earth, pamphlet, 1993.

FEDERAL DOCUMENTS

United States Senate Executive Document 73, vol. 2248, 49th Cong., 2d sess.

INDEX

Ball, Eve, 29, 37; angers Dahteste, 69; as author of *Indeh: An Apache Odyssey*, 97*n* 1

Carlisle Indian School, 30–32
Chihuahua, Eugene: son of Chief Chihuahua, 97*n* 2
Child-of-the-Water, 38; in creation myth, 3–6; as son of Ussen, 5
children and infants: behavior of, 25; birth traditions for, 20; and education during imprisonment, 27–32; first haircuts for, 22; first moccasins for, 22; and learning through storytelling, 23–25, 27; naming ceremony for, 20; puberty ceremony for, 33–40; traditional training of, 26
children's formal education: acquired diseases during, 30–31, 102*n* 26; at Carlisle School, 29–32; at Fort Marion, 27–29; at Hampton Normal and Industrial Institute, Virginia, 101*n* 16
Cleghorn, Mildred Imach (1910–97): and adoption of Penny, 83; and allotments, 106*n* 3; Apache, Oklahoma, brief history of, 80; and attitude toward lost traditions, 93; as Chairperson of Fort Sill Chiricahua/Warm Springs Apache Tribe, xi, 92; and dance attire, xvi; death of, 94; and depicting imprisonment experience, 89–90; description of, 88; and dollmaking,

83–88; and doll's clothing, traditional Chiricahua Apache, 79; education of, 81–82; as 1989 Indian of the Year, xi, 90; as extension agent in Kansas, Oklahoma, and New Mexico, 82–83; farm chores of, 81; funeral of, 95; and George Wratten, 105–106*n* 1; as Honored One at 1990 Red Earth, 91–92; marries to Bill Cleghorn, 83; at Mescalero Apache Reservation, xv; on mother's dollmaking, 79; parents and grandparents of, 77; as prisoner of war, 78–79; professional life of, 82–83; at puberty ceremony, 36; and relation to author, xiv; on release from imprisonment, 79–80; religious affiliation of, 92; retirement of, 93–94; significant achievements of, 94; and tanning a hide, 17; and view of religion, 93
Coyote: in children's story, 23; in creation myth, 5; description of, 4
cradleboard, 20, 21, 22
creation myths: definition of, 3; and examples of Chiricahua Apache, 3–6; Geronimo's favorite, 5; variety of, 3

Dahteste (Old Lady Coonie), 69–70; death and burial of, 104*n* 12
Daklugie, Asa: on puberty ceremony, 37; as son of Nednhi Apache Chief Juh, 97*n* 2
Darrow, Ruey, xi

36–37; initiated by maiden, 8; Mountain Spirit dancers (*Gah'e*) at, 38; preparations for, 33–34; purpose of, 33; ritual markings in, 34